WALKS IN
PEAK NATIONAL PARK

by
Peter and Pat Tidsall

18 circular footpath walks of 6 to 12 miles

FOLLOW THE COUNTRY CODE

Guard against all risk of fire
Fasten all gates
Keep dogs under proper control
Keep to paths across farmland
Avoid damaging fences, hedges and walls
Leave no litter
Safeguard water supplies
Protect wildlife, wild plants and trees
Go carefully on country roads
Respect the life of the countryside

The route maps are reproduced by permission of Ordnance Survey on behalf of The Controller of Her Majesty's Stationery Office, © Crown Copyright 100018979.

Printed in Great Britain.

ISBN 0 85100 124 6

DERBYSHIRE COUNTRYSIDE LIMITED
Heritage House, Lodge Lane, Derby, DE1 3HE

INDEX OF WALKS

2

INDEX OF WALKS

Possible refreshment stops are underlined. On four of the walks there are no available Public Houses or cafes on the route and therefore picnic areas have been suggested.

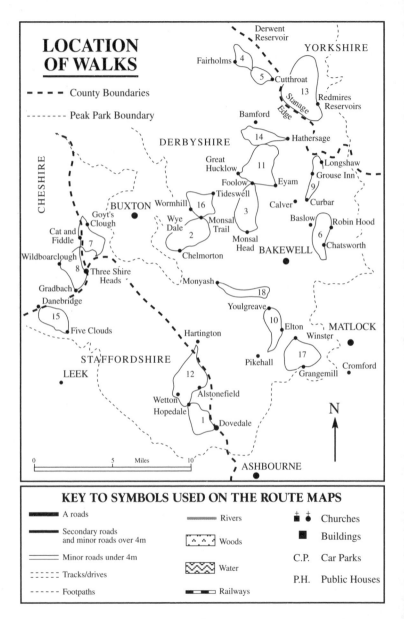

LOCATION OF WALKS

- - - County Boundaries

------- Peak Park Boundary

Derwent Reservoir

YORKSHIRE

Fairholms 4

5 Cutthroat

13 Redmires Reservoirs

Stanage Edge

Bamford

DERBYSHIRE

14 Hathersage

Great Hucklow

11 Longshaw

Foolow Eyam Grouse Inn

Tideswell 9

CHESHIRE

BUXTON

Wormhill 16 3 Calver Curbar

Wye Dale Monsal Trail Baslow Robin Hood

Goyt's Clough 2 Monsal Head 6 Chatsworth

Cat and Fiddle 7 Chelmorton BAKEWELL

Wildboarclough

8 Three Shire Heads

Gradbach Monyash 18

Danebridge

15 Five Clouds Youlgreave

10 Elton MATLOCK

Winster

Hartington Pikehall 17 Cromford

STAFFORDSHIRE Grangemill

LEEK 12

Wetton Alstonefield

Hopedale 1 Dovedale N

0   5   Miles   10

ASHBOURNE

KEY TO SYMBOLS USED ON THE ROUTE MAPS

▬▬▬ A roads	▬▬▬ Rivers	✝ ● Churches
▬▬ Secondary roads and minor roads over 4m	Woods	■ Buildings
═══ Minor roads under 4m	Water	C.P. Car Parks
:::::: Tracks/drives		P.H. Public Houses
------ Footpaths	▬▬ Railways	

4

Introduction

The Peak National Park, covering most of North Derbyshire and extending to Staffordshire, Cheshire and South Yorkshire, is one of the most popular walking areas in the country. The medium-length walks in this book visit a great variety of landscapes - open expanses of dramatic moorland, deep silent valleys, extensive reservoirs, wide meandering rivers, small gurgling streams, impressive gritstone edges and many historically interesting villages. From May to September you will have a chance to see some of the famous well dressings. North Derbyshire was intensively worked in Roman times for lead, limestone and gritstone and on most of the walks you will see the evidence. Earlier human activity shows up in stone circles and prehistoric remains. The bookshops in most of the towns and villages of the Peak District have a good selection of books describing the area.

All the walks are along statutory footpaths and bridlepaths. It is advisable to wear stout footwear, ideally, boots and thick woollen socks, in view of the rocky and sometimes muddy terrain. The weather in North Derbyshire can be very unpredictable and warm waterproof clothing should be part of your equipment; remember, as you climb higher, the temperature drops. A sketch map is provided for each walk but it is useful to have the O.S. 25,000 maps of the Peak District. The new Explorer maps OL. 24 and OL. 1 are replacing the outdoor leisure maps.

The O.S. Touring map Peak District & Derbyshire 3 inches-to-5 miles will help you find the towns and villages from which directions are given to the start of each walk.

Please note the route instructions after crossing stiles or through gates are given as you stand with your back to the stile you have just crossed. These walks were all revised in 2002. However when following any walk route you will find changes to the details described e.g. gates may become gateways, or visa versa, signposts added or removed, stiles changed to gates. Similarly the time of the year can alter the appearance of a path; after heavy rain there will be an increase of mud and stepping-stones will be more difficult where the rivers and streams increase in height. All this adds to the excitement and interest of walking.

If you have enjoyed the walks in the two short walks books *Circular Walks in the Peak Park* and *Short Walks in the Peak Park*, why not now try these somewhat longer walks (6-12 miles) which will give you a full day's walk with a refreshment stop about halfway and time to enjoy the glorious countryside.

ILAM - DOVEDALE

Dovedale Car Park - Ilam - Manifold Valley - Castern Hall - Hopedale - Stanshope - Hall Dale - Dovedale

MAP: O.S. Explorer OL. 24. The Peak District White Peak Area.

DIRECTIONS:

> From Ashbourne Market take the A515 road to Buxton. Half-a mile past the derestriction sign turn left onto the Thorpe, Ilam, Dovedale road. In two miles turn left signed again Thorpe, Ilam, Dovedale. Pass the *Peveril of the Peak Hotel* and then drive through Thorpe village staying on the same road. Drive down into Dovedale, where the views are breathtaking. Cross the Dove then turn sharp right signed 'Car Park' passing the entrance to the *Izaak Walton Hotel.* In quarter-of-a-mile turn into the car park. Grid ref. S.K. 146509.

WALK DESCRIPTION: No walk book would be complete without a visit to the famous Dovedale. The walk starts with an easy stroll across the fields behind the *Izaak Walton Hotel* to the hamlet of Ilam. The Gothic cross in the centre of Ilam near the bridge was erected in memory of Mrs. Watts-Russell; her name is given to the public house in Hopedale where you can pause for refreshments. From Ilam Hall, now a *National Trust* property, the walk follows the elusive Manifold which has two courses - one along a subterranean route through an underground lake regaining its overland course beneath the limestone cliffs in the grounds of the Hall; the other above ground. At the end of the riverside path you will follow the drive up round Castern Hall, home of the Hurt family, and on to Hopedale, crossing an old lead mining area. The return route from the small hamlet of Hopedale is down the beautiful dry valley of Hall Dale and then on down the popular and magnificent Dovedale.

ROUTE INSTRUCTIONS:

1. From the car park cross the road and go over a stile, bear left across the over-flow car park then up steps and through trees to cross a stile.
2. Continue ahead up the field passing the *Izaak Walton* on your left. Following field paths crossing three stiles, one gate and three fields.
3. Walk down a wide track and in about 100 metres bear left down to the road passing through a gate. Turn right into Ilam.
4. At the monument, turn right and walk up to the *National Trust* property of Ilam Hall. Before reaching the entrance turn left signed 'Church' then left again through a gate signed 'Footpath to Church & Hall'. Follow the driveway, then turn up the path with the fence and church on your left, go through a small gate.

Turn left in front of the Hall. Walk down the steps and turn right then fork left down to the river.

5. Turn right to follow the river path keeping the meandering Manifold river on your left. Notice *The Battle Stone* on your right. Having walked about half-a-mile along the valley cross a stile by a gate.

6. Continue ahead still following the river on your left. You will cross a metal stile then further on 2 wooden stiles. This stretch is nearly half a mile.

7. Turn left along the road for a few metres then fork right to follow the Castern Farms driveway as it winds its way uphill.

8. Follow the metal fence on your left round Castern Hall then the waymarked route round the back of the Hall to cross the cattle grid.

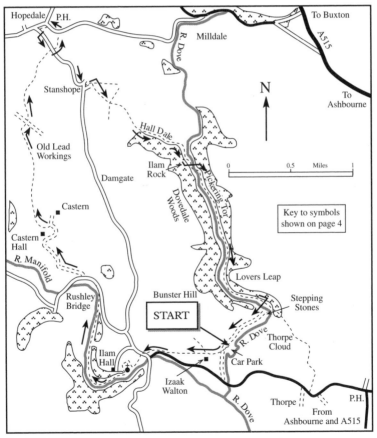

7

9. After crossing the cattle grid bear left off the track where it bends right and shortly cross a stile by a gate.
10. Follow a wide track keeping the wall down on your left. Cross a stile by a gate and keep straight on up the field still with the wall on your left to cross another stile by a gate. Bear right away from the wall to follow a half-embanked grass track up the undulating field heading for the right-hand gate on the skyline.
11. Cross the stile by the gate and keep straight on up the field veering away very slightly left and passing a small mound on your left. Go through the gate.
12. Keep straight on for a few metres then turn right along a grass track with a wall on your left and old spoil heaps on your right.
13. At a tall metal signpost cross two squeeze stiles and a lane to follow the 'Public Footpath to Hopedale' sign. Bear left across the field to go through a stile.
14. Keep straight on crossing four fields and four stiles with a wall on your left. In the fourth field, where the wall bends left, keep straight on to cross the stile in the field corner.
15. Keep straight on across the next field to go through a squeeze stile then follow a wall close on your right. Cross a squeeze stile and turn right to Stanshope. (If you want refreshments at *The Watts Russell Arms* cross the minor road, go through the squeeze stile and bear left down a small valley to the road. Go over a stile and turn left along the road to the inn. After your refreshments follow the steep narrow path up the hill opposite the inn, then turn left along the road to Stanshope.)
16. At Stanshope Hall follow the road round to the right and in a few yards at a Footpath sign turn left down a lane to Milldale. In about 70 metres turn right signed 'Public Footpath to Dovedale via Halldale'.
17. Cross the field corner and go over a stile on your left, then bear right to cross a gated stile near the field corner. Continue ahead keeping a wall on your right and <u>passing</u> a stile on your right. Cross two more stiles.
18. Enter the National Trust Hall Dale. Walk down the beautiful dry valley of Hall Dale crossing two stiles.
19. On reaching the Dove turn right over a wall stile and walk along the riverside path. At Ilam Rock cross the footbridge and turn right below Pickering Tor.
20. Walk along the well-used wide Dovedale path following the beautiful river on your right. In the next one-and-a-quarter miles of magnificent limestone dale scenery you will go through 2 gates, 1 stile and climb one hill over Lover's Leap.
21. Cross the stepping stones and turn left down the small riverside road back to the car park. If the stepping stones are flooded follow the left bank of the river then cross the bridge back to the car park.

BAKEWELL - WALK 2   10 MILES

TADDINGTON AND CHELMORTON

**Wye Dale - Chee Dale - Monsal Trail - Priestcliffe - Taddington -
Chelmorton - Horseshoe Dale - Deep Dale -
Topley Pike Quarry - Wye Dale**

MAP: O.S. Explorer OL. 24. The Peak District White Peak Area

DIRECTIONS: From Bakewell take the A6 to Buxton. 2½ miles past Taddington turn right opposite Topley Pike Quarry into the Peak National Park Wyedale car park - Grid Ref. S.K. 104724.

WALK DESCRIPTION: This spectacular 10 mile walk can be shortened to 8 or 6 miles as is shown on the map. We strongly advise walkers to follow this route after a period of dry weather. *The Church Inn* at Chelmorton provides a good refreshment stop for all three routes. From the Wyedale car park the 10 and 6 mile walks follow the easy valley path by the River Wye before ascending to the Monsal Trail. This area still has evidence of early industrial activity. The 6 mile walk leaves the trail in 100 metres to follow paths to Chelmorton. The 10 mile route follows the valley through Chee Dale where stepping stones ford the river below high limestone cliffs, these may be covered after heavy rain. From the dale just past Miller's Dale car park (where the 8 mile route starts) the route climbs via field paths and lanes to the hill-top villages of Taddington and Chelmorton, both old lead mining and farming villages. The return route for the 8 mile walk follows the outward route of the 6 mile walk (see map). From Chelmorton the 10 and 6 mile walks follow a wide grassy bridleway of Horseshoe Dale and then on down the narrow stony and silent Deep Dale where magnificent limestone cliffs tower above the valley floor. The path down Deep Dale may be very difficult especially after rain has made the rocks slippery.

ROUTE INSTRUCTIONS:
1. Leave the car park and follow the 'Bridleway to Monsal Trail' path by the River Wye. Pass under two viaducts. Just before the third viaduct turn right up steps signed Monsal Trail.
2. Follow the trail for just over 1 mile noticing the impressive limestone cliffs. Ignore the Chee Dale paths. Walk through 2 tunnels.
3. Where the trail ends in a sealed-off tunnel turn right over a stile to follow the Miller's Dale/Wye Dale path down to the river turning right to follow the Miller's Dale route. Pass under the line of the old railway then cross a footbridge over the Wye.

9

4. Follow the very varied riverside path first over stepping stones (take care) then eventually over a footbridge, a stile and another footbridge crossing tributary streams. Continue along the riverside path which in places climbs up limestone slabs. At a bridge over the Wye bear left (do not cross it) and continue along the river path. At the viaduct turn left up steps signed 'Monsal Trail'. At the top turn left.

5. Follow the Trail to walk through the Miller's Dale car park. At the end of the old station buildings turn right through a gate then left to follow the Trail for about 450 metres. Turn right off the Trail to follow a path up steps over a stile and up the very steep path ahead.

6. On reaching a wall ahead follow it on your left for a few yards then cross it via a stone stile. Continue ahead across the middle of the next field to go through a squeeze stile.

7. Continue in more or less the same direction crossing six fields and six stiles.

8. After crossing the sixth stile turn right to cross the corner of the next field to go over a stile by a signpost in the adjacent wall. Turn left along the farm lane for a few yards. At the road junction in Priestcliffe turn right and in about 50 metres bear left downhill on a surfaced lane. Follow this undulating lane for just over $^1/_2$ mile.

9. Cross the A6 dual carriageway and continue straight on through the outskirts of Taddington, following a narrow road and crossing two wider roads, walk up Slipperlow Lane.

10. Just past the last building on the right, turn right over a stile signposted 'Public Footpath to Chelmorton 2'. Keep straight on up the field crossing a broken wall and on up to a signpost and crossing another broken wall. Continue uphill towards the right-hand clump of trees on the skyline.

11. Cross a wall stile by a footpath post and bear right towards the mound of Sough Top Reservoir and a gate in the field corner. Cross the high wall stile. Bear right across the next field towards a post on the horizon.

12. Cross a stile by a gate. Continue in the same direction crossing six undulating fields and six stiles. Cross a track and a stile, then cross another four fields and four stiles. Keep a wall on your right except in the last field and pass *Five Wells Farm* on your right.

13. Walk diagonally right across a lane to go through a squeeze stile on your left. Follow a well-defined path through the tussock grass of an old lead working area. The path eventually leads into a walled track that takes you down into Chelmorton Village.

14. Walk down the village road passing the church on your left (notice the 'golden' grasshopper on top of the weather vane) and *The Church Inn* on your right. In about 140 metres turn right at a signpost.

15. Follow the lane passing *Shepley Farm* on your right. At the end of the walled lane pass through a gateway and turn immediately left down a

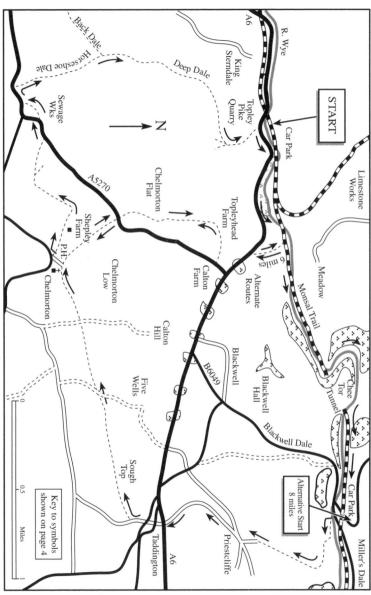

Crown Copyright Reserved

11

grassed, gated and walled track crossing a minor road part way down. Follow this track round a right-hand corner then almost immediately go over a stile on your left.

16. Bear right across the field to a gateway in the opposite wall. Continue ahead along a stony walled track passing through the right-hand gateway then over a stile by a gate.

17. On reaching the road turn left. Walk past the Severn Trent Water installation and where the road bends left, turn right over a stile by the Severn Trent Water boundary fence.

18. Walk slightly diagonally left up the field towards a small mound and cross a stile in the opposite wall. Walk up the next field keeping a wall on your left, cross a wall stile in the field corner.

19. Turn right down the road for nearly 180 metres. At the bottom of the hill turn right signed 'Public Bridleway' and go through a small gate. Walk through the farmyard then through the farm gate.

20. Walk down the beautiful grassy Horseshoe Dale for just over half-a-mile. This is an ideal picnic area. At the junction with Back Dale keep straight on into the narrower, rocky and silent Deep Dale.

21. In just over one mile at the end of the Dale cross a stile, walk up a wider track by the slurry area, at the end of which the path narrows and descends very steeply to the valley bottom.

22. Cross a broken wall and turn left to follow the path, with a fence and the quarry workings on your left, to the main road. Cross the A6 back to the Wyedale car park.

BAKEWELL - WALK 3   8¹/₂ MILES

MONSAL HEAD

Monsal Head - Monsal Trail - Cressbrook Dale - Foolow - Housley House - Longstone Moor - Little Longstone - Monsal Head

MAP: O.S. Explorer OL. 24. The Peak District White Peak Area.

DIRECTIONS: From Bakewell take the A6 Buxton road. In just over 1¹/₂ miles turn right onto the A6020 into Ashford-in-the-Water, in 230 metres turn left onto the B6465 Wardlow Monsal Head road. Follow this road for 1¹/₄ miles. Turn left into the pay and display car park at Monsal Head. Parking. Grid Ref. S.K. 185715.

WALK DESCRIPTION: Monsal Head, the starting point of this walk, is a famous viewpoint overlooking Monsal Dale and the viaduct which carries the

Trail, the first section of your walk. At the end of the trail the route passes through the old mill village of Cressbrook then up and down the picturesque limestone dale of Cressbrook passing Peter's Stone (said to be named after St. Peter's in Rome). After crossing the A623 the walk follows field paths and lanes to Foolow where *The Bulls Head* provides a halfway refreshment stop. The return route is due south across field and moorland paths.

ROUTE INSTRUCTIONS:

1. From the car park walk between the two parts of the *Monsal Head Hotel*. Turn left on the road and walk to the larger opening in a low stone wall opposite the *Monsal View* cafe. Go through and turn right.

2. Descend the valley via shallow stone steps. A short way down turn left signed 'Viaduct and Monsal Trail'. Continue downhill to the trail. Go through a gate and turn right.

3. Follow the Monsal Trail for just over one mile. Notice the plaques for Monsal Dale Station and Cressbrook Mill. By the latter the trail leaves the disused railway and contours the hillside before descending stone steps to cross a footbridge over the River Wye by the weir.

4. After crossing the river bear right leaving the Monsal Trail. Follow the path round the converted mill buildings.

5. Turn left at the road and in a few metres bear right uphill signed 'Cressbrook and Litton 2'.

6. In just over $1/4$ mile fork right down a surfaced lane signed 'Ravensdale no through road'. Pass cottages on your right and follow a narrow path by the 'Public Footpath' sign.

7. Follow the dale path uphill ignoring a path off to the left and keeping to the main path with an old wall on your right.

8. Cross a footbridge. Shortly the path starts to climb up away from the river.

9. At the top of the dale, by an *English Nature* footpath sign, bear left and descend into the dale on a steep, well-defined partly stepped path.

10. Walk up the dale, keeping a wall on your left, for about $3/4$ mile. Notice the impressive Peter's Stone up on your right.

11. At the end of the dale keep a wall close on your right, ignoring a path on your left. Go through a gate and walk behind the buildings to turn down left to the road. Turn right along the A623.

12. Cross the entrance to the Wardlow road, then opposite the car park and transport café turn left across the road.

13. Walk down the short farm drive. Turn left and follow the footpath signs round the farm buildings. Go through a small gate then follow the line of the wall on your left.

14. Cross a wall stile and continue to follow the wall up the next field to cross another stile by a gate. Bear left up the next field towards a house. Cross a stile by a gate.

15. Turn right and walk along the farm track passing Stanley House on your right. In about 375 metres the track bends left; you keep straight on down a narrower walled track crossing the end of Silly Dale.

16. At the bottom of the track, leave it to cross a stile by the footpath sign on your left.

17. Walk up the field keeping a wall on your right and go through a wall gap.

18. Continue in the same direction crossing 9 fields and stiles, 1 track and 1 gate. The fourth field is very small and in the fifth field you will walk diagonally left

19. After the gate in the ninth field bear right down the next field to go through another gate. Follow a track and a path down into Foolow.

20. From *The Bulls Head* cross the main road and walk down the Wardlow Middleton road keeping to the right-hand side for just over a quarter of a mile.

21. Fork right signed 'Buxton Manchester (A6)' and separate signs 'Housley' and 'Wardlow'. Walk down to the A623 and cross the road to go over a stile on your right.

22. Turn left and walk down the field passing a house on your left. Cross a fence stile, a field with a wall on the left and a stile by a gate.

23. Bear diagonally right across the field and go over a wall stile. Cross the next field and pass through a flapped stile in the right hand corner.

24. Walk past a wood on your left, shortly bear right away from the wood across the field to go over a fence stile in the field corner. Cross the farm drive, over a wall stile and bear right across the next field to go through a wall stile.

25. Cross a minor road and go over a small ladder stile. Walk up the field diagonally left aiming for a point about three-quarters of the way along a wall on your left. (Do not go as far as the single tree.) Cross a wall stile by a small red waymarked sign.

26. Bear right and cross a wall stile about 50 metres up from the single tree and the field corner.

27. Continue ahead crossing 7 fields, 5 stiles, 1 track, 2 small gates and a broken wall.

28. Cross the road and the stile by a footpath sign. Continue in the same southerly direction crossing 2 fields and stiles. In the third field you will have a wall on your right for a short way then another wall on your right as you near the end of the field. Cross the stile in the field corner.

29. On reaching the open moorland of Longstone Moor bear slightly left following the narrow undulating path which shortly winds its way through the heather. In nearly $1/2$ mile pass a 'Footpath' sign still following the path now downhill, across a raised path and then ascend gradually. The path narrows for a short distance as it follows the line of a trench then Watersaw Rake on your right.

30. On reaching Black Plantation on your right follow the line of the fence on

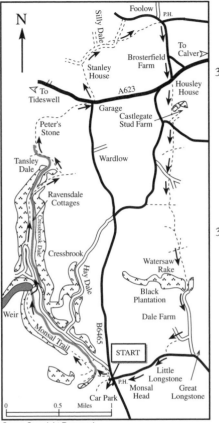

N

Foolow
P.H.
Silly Dale
To
Calver
Brosterfield
Farm
Stanley
House
Housley
House
A623
To
Tideswell
Garage
Castlegate
Stud Farm
Peter's
Stone
Wardlow
Tansley
Dale
Ravensdale
Cottages
Cressbrook Dale
Cressbrook
Hay Dale
Watersaw
Rake
B6465
Black
Plantation
Weir
Dale Farm
Monsal Trail
START
Little
Longstone
P.H.
Monsal
Head
Great
Longstone
Car Park

0   0.5   1
Miles

Crown Copyright Reserved

your right until you cross a stile by a gate. Bear left to follow the steep winding path down through the wood.

31. Cross a track at the bottom of the steps and keep straight on down the path to go through a wooden gate. Walk down the minor road for about 450 metres and turn right signed 'Dale Farm'. Walk up the lane. Just past the farm on your right and where the lane turns sharp right keep straight on to cross a stile.

32. Cross the field keeping a wall close on your left. Cross a wall stile. Just past a house on your left cross a stile by a gate on your left. Walk down the wide grass track to the road. Turn right and follow the road through Little Longstone back to the car park at Monsal Head.

Key to symbols
shown on page 4

BAMFORD - WALK 4   7½ MILES

DERWENT EDGE

**Fairholms Car Park - Derwent Dam and Reservoir -
Walker's Clough - Derwent Edge -
Grindle Clough - Wellhead - Fairholms**

MAP: O.S. Explorer OL. 1. Peak District Dark Peak Area.

DIRECTIONS: From Bamford follow the A6013 north for 2 miles to cross the viaduct over the Ladybower reservoir. Turn left onto

15

the A57 signposted 'Glossop'. In just over $\frac{1}{2}$ mile turn right up the reservoir road signposted 'Derwent Valley'. In $2\frac{1}{2}$ miles turn right into the Fairholms car park. Grid Ref. S.K. 173893. This car park could be crowded at Bank Holidays and fine weekends.

WALK DESCRIPTION: You need to be energetic and to choose a clear cool day preferably in the spring or autumn to derive maximum benefit from this walk. The area covered illustrates Derbyshire at its most dramatic. We start with an easy stroll along the side of the Derwent Reservoir before a long steep climb of 350m up onto Derwent Edge. As you walk along the Edge you will see the effects of erosion which have produced sculptured gritstone rock formations like the Salt Cellar and the Wheel Stones. This $1\frac{3}{4}$ mile edge path provides stimulating views across the Kinder Plateau. The return route descends from the Derwent Edge to the Ladybower Reservoir where the remains of the drowned Derwent village can sometimes be seen at low water. Refreshments can be had at the Fairholms Visitor Centre where you can park the car.

ROUTE INSTRUCTIONS:

1. From the car park return to the Visitor Centre and turn right opposite it at the 'Footpath to Derwent Dam' sign. Follow this path to the minor road ignoring a path off to the right. Turn right along the road to go over a bridge. Walk below the dam and just before the end of the dam turn left off the road to follow a wide grass path to the dam. Turn right up steps to the top of the dam. Turn left to follow a woodland path. Go through a small gate .

2. Follow the unmade road with the reservoir on your left. In just over $\frac{1}{2}$ mile turn right signposted 'Public Footpath to Bradfield and Strines'.

3. Climb the steep well-defined path uphill onto the moors following all footpath and waymarked signs. Near the top at a signpost keep straight on up.

4. In about 230 metres on meeting a broken wall ahead turn right with that wall on your left. On reaching a ladder stile cross it and keep straight on signed 'Public Footpath Strines'.

5. Follow the wide moorland path; in a few metres another path joins it on the right. Continue ahead following this path for about 275 metres then bear right on a slightly less defined path towards the top of the ridge (Lost Lad).

6. Follow this path which shortly crosses a footbridge and bends round to the right then starts to climb diagonally up the ridge.

7. Near the top and just after a steeper section the path bears left below a low outcrop of gritstone.

16

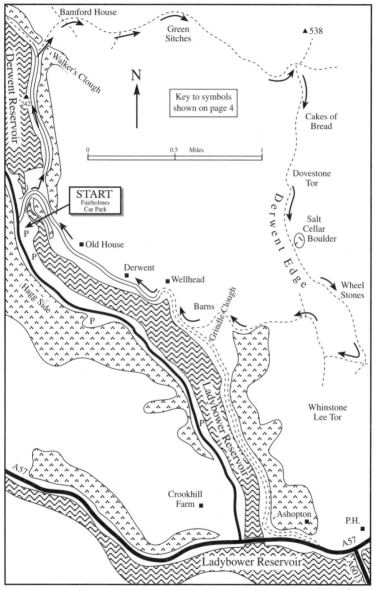

17

8. At the top of the ridge by the boundary stone turn right to follow the well-used path along Derwent Edge. (Please keep to the National Trust path.) You will pass many interesting rock formations as shown on the map. The total distance along the edge is about 1³/₄ miles. Up here the views across to Lose Hill, Hollins Cross, Mam Tor, Rushup Edge and over Edale Moor and the Kinder Plateau are magnificent.

9. At the distinctive pillar of rock, The Salt Cellar, continue to follow the edge path passing a small pool on your left, then on to pass the impressive rocks of the Wheel Stones on the horizon

10. In nearly 450 metres past the Wheel Stones rocks turn right at a 'Public Footpath to Derwent and Moscar' sign.

11. Follow the moorland path quite steeply downhill. At a wall in front of you turn right and follow the wall on your left until you reach a gate.

12. Turn left down the 'Bridleway' signed 'Derwent'. On reaching a wall corner cross a stile by a gate and continue on down with a conifer wood on your left. Just beyond the wood go through a small gate to enter The National Trust High Peak Estate *High House Farm*.

13. Follow the path on downhill to pass through another gate, across a stream, over a stile by a gate and walk round the 350 year old barns in Grindle Clough. Go through a small gate by the barns.

14. Follow the steep path downhill which shortly bends right, down to the field corner where you go through a gate.

15. Turn right along the unsurfaced road above the reservoir on your left. At Wellhead just before joining the minor road notice the 'Upper Derwent Valley' notice-board describing the position of the drowned village of Derwent.

16. Join the surfaced road and follow it back to Derwent dam for just over 1 mile and so round to the Fairholms car park.

BAMFORD - WALK 5   6 MILES

LADYBOWER RESERVOIR

Derwent Moors - Whinstone Lee Tor - Grindle Clough - Ladybower Reservoir - Cutthroat Bridge

MAP: O.S. Explore OL. 1. The Peak District Dark Peak Area.

DIRECTIONS: From Bamford follow the A6013 north to cross the viaduct. Turn right onto the A57 Sheffield road. In just over one mile after passing Cutthroat Bridge turn into a lay-by car park on your right.

PARKING: In the lay-by. Grid ref. S.K. 216874.

DESCRIPTION: On this walk you will be rewarded with superb views for very little effort. The first stretch across open moorland leads to a fine viewpoint at Whinstone Lee Tor. In the middle distance the twin humps of Crook Hill, then Win Hill beyond; in the distance is Losehill and Mam Tor; beyond Edale Valley is the elongated Kinder Scout Plateau. From this viewpoint the walk continues along the moor above the Ladybower Reservoir eventually to descend the hillside and following roads, paths and bridleways round the reservoir back to your starting point. The *Ladybower Inn* is a suitable refreshment stop.

HISTORY: The name Cut-throat was given to the bridge on the A57 by local inhabitants in the 16th century when a man was found in the area having been fatally wounded to the throat and face by robbers and footpads. Seven miles north of Bamford the first reservoir was started in 1901. The Ladybower Reservoir required the inundation of two villages - Derwent and Ashopton. When the water is *very* low, remains can be seen.

ROUTE INSTRUCTIONS:

1. Turn left out of the lay-by and walk down the road for about 180 metres. Cross Cutthroat Bridge and immediately turn right through a gate.
2. Follow the main moorland bridleway, which soon bears left, in a steady gentle ascent for just over 1 mile. At first you will have a fence on the right.
3. At a crossing of six paths near Whinstone Lee Tor turn right at the 'Bridleway' sign and walk below the outcrop of rocks.
4. Follow the path across the moor keeping a wall close on your left for nearly one mile.
5. At a gateway turn left, signposted 'Derwent', and walk down the moorland bearing slightly right towards a conifer wood.
6. Pass through a gate and continue downhill with a conifer wood on your left and a wall on your right. Eventually bear away right from the wood to pick up a wall on your left.
7. Go through a gate and continue to follow the wall on your left, walking down a rocky path to go through another gateway.
8. Cross a stream and follow a path to go through another gateway. The path now passes between barns turning left to go through a small gate at the end of the barn.
9. Follow the stone and slab path downhill with a wall and a fence on your right at first. Pass through a small gate.
10. Turn left along the reservoir track. In about ¼ mile go through a gate and follow the track round a hairpin bend.

11. In about one mile pass through a small gate and fork left up a tarmac road, passing houses on your right.
12. Keep straight on at the edge of the wood to pass through a gate and then another gate up ahead of you.
13. Walk along a narrow undulating bracken-edged path with the reservoir and shortly a wall on your right.
14. Eventually pass through a gate and walk behind the *Ladybower Inn*. Join a wide track and bear left uphill.
15. Pass through another gate to enter the *Derbyshire Wild Life Trust* Nature Reserve and continue uphill.
16. Where the path forks, keep straight on to follow the 'Footpath' sign. Continue ahead towards and under power lines.
17. Cross a stream and go through a gate. Follow the moorland bridleway. At a fork of paths bear right to reach your outward path. Turn right back to Cutthroat Bridge and the lay-by.

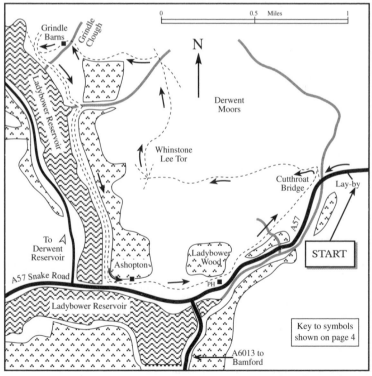

Crown Copyright Reserved

BASLOW - WALK 6   9¹/₂ **MILES**

CHATSWORTH

Chatsworth Park - Baslow - Yeld Wood - Gardom's Edge - Dobb Edge - Chatsworth Woods and Moors - Beeley Lodge - Calton Lees

MAP: O.S. Explorer OL. 24. The Peak District White Peak Area

DIRECTIONS: From Baslow take the A619 Bakewell road; where this road turns right keep straight on to drive through Chatsworth Park. At the second cattle grid turn right into Calton Lees car park.

DESCRIPTION: This is a very varied scenic walk with wonderful views from Gardom's and Dobb's Edges (both ideal picnic sites). The walk starts through Chatsworth Park to Baslow. Then you climb gradually up the road, through Yeld Wood and on up to Gardom's Edge. From the Edge to the A619 follow the more obvious of the moorland paths. The Dobb's Edge concessionary path leads to the last part of the walk through Chatsworth Woods and moorland.

ROUTE INSTRUCTIONS:

1. Leave the car park via the vehicular entrance using the 'Footpath to Chatsworth House 1¹/₄ miles' path. Go through the gate and cross the road.
2. Keep straight on down the field ignoring the path bearing left. Turn left at the river. Follow the riverside path.
3. On reaching Chatsworth Bridge turn right across it then immediately left. Go through a small gate.
4. Follow the path through Chatsworth Park for ³/₄ mile ignoring all paths off right and left. Go through a tall circular gate and continue ahead on a wide walled and hedged path to Baslow.
5. At the road junction turn left over the bridge and keep straight on at the road junction for a few metres to go through the second wall gap and across the main road.
6. Walk up Eaton Hill road for nearly ¹/₄ mile. At the T-junction turn right up Bar road.
7. In about 230 metres, before the 'No motor vehicles...' sign, turn right up a rough road between houses (Moor Cottage is on your left as you enter this road).
8. In a short distance go through a small gate and bear right on the lower

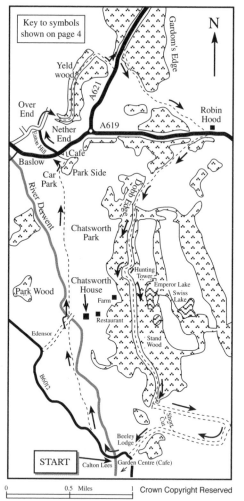

Key to symbols shown on page 4

N

Gardom's Edge

Yeld wood

A621

Over End

Nether End

A619

Robin Hood

Eaton Hill

Baslow

Cafe

Car Park

Park Side

River Derwent

Dobb Edge

Chatsworth Park

Park Wood

Chatsworth House

Hunting Tower

Emperor Lake

Swiss Lake

Farm

Restaurant

Edensor

Stand Wood

B6012

Short Cut

Beeley Lodge

START

Calton Lees

Garden Centre (Cafe)

0   0.5 Miles   1   Crown Copyright Reserved

path, keeping a garden fence on your right.

9. In about 140 metres, opposite a small garden gate, bear left uphill through the woods. Keep to the woodland path. There are some boggy stretches along this route.

10. Eventually you enter a pine plantation.

11. After about ³/₄ mile at the end of the wood go through a small gate and turn right down the field keeping a wall on your right. Cross the footbridge.

12. Bear slightly right to follow the wide track uphill. Cross the wall stile onto the A621 and turn left and walk up the left-hand side of the road

13. In about 180 metres, just past *Cupola Cottage* on your right, cross the road and go over a stile by a water trough.

14. Follow the path uphill, cross another stile and continue ahead with a fence on your right. Shortly the path bears left uphill, away from the fence corner, towards Gardom's Edge.

15. Follow the path uphill for about ¹/₂ mile, you will pass through 1 small and 1 large old wall gap. At the top go through a gate or gateway.

16. Continue ahead keeping a wood down on your right. Soon the path bears left, away from the woodland. Cross a more open area free of bracken. Follow the wide grass path down to the A619.

17. Cross the stile and turn left along the A619. (Should you wish to visit the *Robin Hood Inn* continue along the main road for a few metres.) In about 30 metres cross the road (take care) to a sign 'Do not climb trees...etc'. Cross the stile and follow the stone path and steps downhill. Cross the footbridge. Bear slightly right up the path then climb up shallow steps.

18. Cross a wide stone track and turn right following the 'Beeley via Swiss Lake' path. Cross the ladder stile and turn left uphill.

19. Follow the waymarked concession footpath across Dobb Edge crossing 3 stiles until you reach a high wall stile.

20. Cross this stile and bear slightly left uphill towards a high wall. Continue uphill keeping the wall on your left.

21. Cross another high wall stile and turn left. In a few yards turn right onto a wide woodland track. Keep straight on at a meeting of tracks. Stay on this track until you reach a T-junction. Turn right.

22. Follow the road keeping the Hunting Tower up on your left. Go up the steps on your left to the Tower. Pass in front of the Tower and opposite a sunken door turn right to follow a narrow mauve waymarked path through the woods, ignoring side paths, for about $1/2$ mile.

23. Climb a short flight of steps above the Cascade waterfalls. With your back to the waterfalls climb the steps to the main track and turn right.

24. Follow the track for half-a-mile, and on joining a surfaced drive turn left. At a crossroads of tracks turn right signposted 'Hob Hurst's House Beeley'.

25. Cross a stile by a gate and keep straight on along a wide moorland track for nearly 1 mile. (If you want a short cut turn right at a waymarked post about 130 metres from the wood to join the longer route at instruction 27.)

26. Cross a stile by a gate and turn right down a stony track to meet the shorter walk in about $3/4$ mile.

27. Continue down the track which soon becomes a minor road. At the road junction turn right. After crossing the bridge bear left up through trees back to the car park.

BUXTON - WALK 7 9¹/₂ **MILES**

GOYT VALLEY - AXE EDGE

Goyt's Clough Quarry - Goyt's Clough - Derbyshire Bridge - Axe Edge - Orchard Farm - Danebower Quarries - Danebower Hollow - Cat & Fiddle - Stake Side - Goyt's Clough Quarry

MAP:　　　　O.S. Explorer OL. 24. The Peak District White Peak Area.

PARKING:　　Grid Ref. S.K. 012734

DIRECTIONS: From Buxton take the A5004 to Whaley Bridge. In two miles turn left signed 'Goyt Valley'. In just over 1 mile cross the top of Errwood Reservoir and turn left. Follow the reservoir road for about 1¹/₂ miles to park in the third car park, Goyt's Clough Quarry, which is by a 'No through way' sign.

WALK DESCRIPTION: It is advisable to choose a clear day to follow this very varied walk as part of it crosses the high wild Axe Edge Moor where mists can form quite quickly. From the car park you travel along the pleasant Goyt Valley before crossing Axe Edge Moor. As you approach Orchard Farm you may find new direction signs as the farm is being renovated. The route continues through the disused Danebower Quarries before crossing the A54. The Danebower Hollow track leads to the *Cat & Fiddle Inn*; a suitable refreshment stop. From here you continue to follow the moorland paths, which eventually lead back to the car park via the riverside path.

ROUTE INSTRUCTIONS:

1. Leave the car park and turn right along the road. Follow this very pretty minor valley road with the Goyt river on your left, for about 1 mile to Derbyshire Bridge.
2. After crossing a cattle grid turn sharp left signed 'Berry Clough'. Walk up the stony track passing the car park on your right. In about 275 metres after left and right shallow bends turn right off the track at a low waymarked footpath signed 'Axe Edge Moor'.
3. Follow a narrow moorland path, walking in a SE direction, for just over 275 metres to meet a broken wall on your right. Continue along the path to pass through a gap in a wall and turn left.
4. Follow the bridleway up the gentle incline keeping the broken wall on your left. In about 550 metres, just after passing a fence stile on your left, turn right. Walk across a very short stretch of rough grass to the main A54 and a footpath sign on the far side.
5. Go over the stile. Keep straight on up the Axe Edge moorland path walking

in a southerly direction. On reaching a broken well on your right (about 375 metres) the path turns left for another 140 metres before joining a wider track.

6. Turn right and follow this wider track for 550 metres. On reaching a minor road turn right for a short way then left at the 'Footpath' sign. This is Dane Head, the source of the River Dane.

7. Follow the moorland track which shortly crosses a small stream (the River Dane) before climbing gradually up to Cheeks Hill (450 metres). Cross a waymarked stile. Bear right and walk across the moorland in a SSW direction to the bridleway.

8. On reaching the bridleway turn right. In nearly half a mile pass through a gate and turn right, then go through a gateway and walk up the farm drive. (The original path is now overgrown so you will need to follow the farm drive through the renovated farmyard of Orchard Farm.)

9. Continue to follow the stony driveway until it bends sharp left downhill; at this point keep straight on following a wide grass path which contours the hillside.

10. At the head of the valley cross an old fence stile. Turn left to follow a path for a short way then cross a stream and follow the line of a fence on your left. This shortly drops away as you contour the hillside; in a few yards you will meet a wall on your left.

11. Follow this wall for about half a mile to the disused quarries.

12. Continue ahead to follow the waymarked signs through the quarries. Turn left to cross a stream then on up to turn left again up a steep quarry path. Continue through and out of the quarry on the main grassy path.

13. Cross a stile by a gate and immediately turn right up a very short steep path to the busy A54. Cross the road to go over the stile back onto the moors.

14. Follow the Danebower Hollow moorland track for nearly 1½ miles to the A537 and *The Cat & Fiddle* public house. About halfway along this bridleway a path joins it from the left. At *The Cat & Fiddle* you can obtain refreshments all day except on Mondays when they close at 4pm.

15. Cross the busy road to the pub and turn left. Walk down the side of the road for about 275 metres and at the three-arrow-bend direction sign bear right off the road up a partly surfaced track to pass by a gate and so onto a wide moorland track.

16. In about another 275 metres the track bends right to continue uphill; shortly you will have a fence on your left.

17. Ignore the footpath signs on your right and keep straight on to go through a small gate. Continue along the moorland track with a wall close on your left. Ignore the Shining Tor route on your left.

18. After about ¾ mile the grass track bears off right signed 'Errwood Reservoir and car parks'. Follow this track downhill, going through a kissing gate, until you reach a crossing of tracks.

19. Turn right signed 'Goyts Clough Quarry'. On reaching the road turn right and in a few yards turn left.

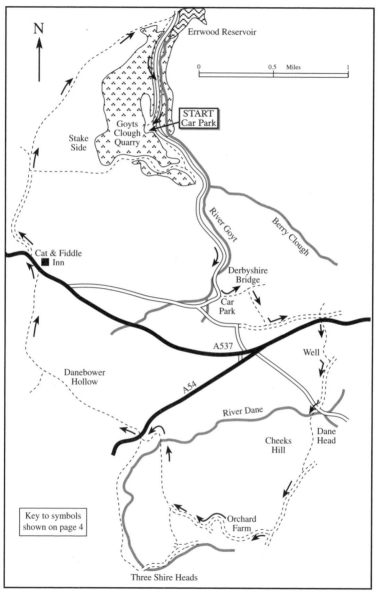

20. Follow the 'Riverside Walk' route for about 375 metres. You will cross three footbridges and climb steps back to the road and car park at Goyts Clough Quarry.

To Return to Buxton: A one-way system operates along the valley road. Leave the car park and turn right, drive along the valley road to Derbyshire Bridge, cross the cattle grid, turn right then first left. At the main A537 turn left to join the A54 into Buxton.

BUXTON - WALK 8   8¹/₂ MILES

**Gradbach car park - Manor Farm -
Three Shire Heads - Dane Valley - Danebower Hollow -
Cumberland Brook - Clough House - Wildboarclough -
A54 - Dane river - Gradbach car park**

MAP: O.S. Explorer OL. 24. White Peak Area and 1-inch-to-1-mile Tourist Map of the Peak District

DIRECTIONS:

From Buxton take the A53 Leek road. In 4¹/₂ miles turn right signed 'Flash' (see map opposite). Follow the minor road, which bears left through Flash, for 2 miles, then bear left again onto a 'no through road' signed 'Peter Watson's Scout Camp Site and Youth Hostel'. In 275 metres turn into the Peak National Park Gradbach car park. Grid Ref. S.J. 998663

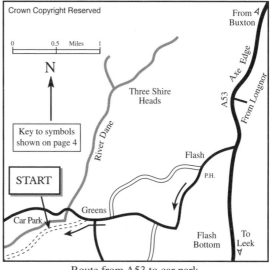

Route from A53 to car park

DESCRIPTION: The Dane river in the Peak District of Derbyshire, Staffordshire and Cheshire flows through very beautiful and wild landscapes. There are many picnic spots but Three Shire Heads where the Derbyshire

Staffordshire and Cheshire boundaries meet is the most popular; here Pannier's Bridge used to be a favourite area in the past for pugilists. *The Crag Inn* at just over ³/₄ way round the route is a suitable refreshment stop. Wildboarclough is said to be so named because the Cumberland Brook in this part of the valley is subject to considerable flooding. We would advise you to do this walk after a period of dry weather.

ROUTE INSTRUCTIONS:
1. From the car park take the waymarked path at the eastern end (i.e. furthest away from the entrance). Follow the grass path, with the river on your left, for about 100 metres. Go through a squeeze stile and immediately turn left over a small footbridge. Bear right and continue to follow the river on your left. In a few metres, after passing under trees, bear right to cross a stile onto the road.
2. Turn right to follow the road for about 75 metres round a left-hand bend then turn left through a gate near a cottage. Bear right uphill to cross a wall stile.
3. Walk up the field towards a gate passing an asbestos and timber house on your left. Pass through the gate and continue up the next four fields passing through gateways, stiles and gates and having a wall close on your left. In the fifth field where the wall stops keep straight on.
4. Cross a stile by a gateway and keep straight on across a reedy pasture towards a gate. Just before this gate turn left along an old grass track to cross a stile by a gate.
5. Keep straight on still following the grass track as it winds round the hill. When you meet a shale track bear left on it. Follow this track as it meanders down the hillside to pass a barn on the left. Here the track turns left downhill to join another track coming in from the left.
6. Continue along the track with the river on your left for a few yards before turning right by a bridge on your left, to follow the Footpath sign. Walk up the stony path keeping the river and shortly a wall on your left.
7. Continue along the well-defined path above the Dane river passing through one gate, until you reach Three Shire Heads. (Instructions 6 & 7 cover nearly ³/₄ mile.)
8. Turn left over the bridge then immediately right to follow the path up the valley.
9. Just before a gate turn right over a stile and follow the path near the river.
10. Where the path meets a marshy area it may be necessary to make a detour up to a higher part of the field before crossing a stile ahead of you at a point where the river meanders. You may have to make another short detour before crossing a broken wall and a stile by a footpath sign in the field corner.
11. The path now follows the river again. Just past a ruined building the path climbs up away from the river, shortly passing an old lead-mining tower.
12. Near the top of the steep climb turn left over the stile by a gate then sharp right to continue up another very short steep path up to the road.
13. Cross the busy road and follow the bridleway, Danebower Hollow onto the moors.

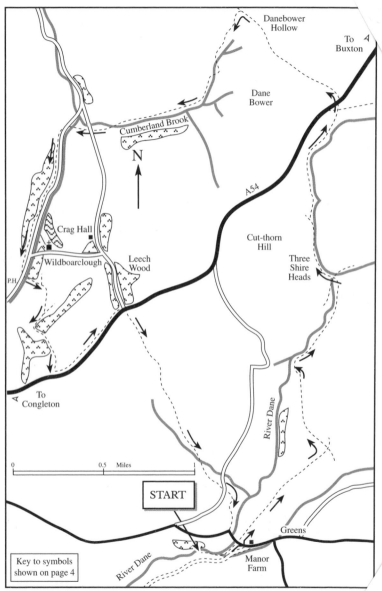

Danebower
Hollow

To
Buxton

Dane
Bower

Cumberland Brook

N

A54

Crag Hall

Cut-thorn
Hill

Wildboarclough

Leech
Wood

Three
Shire
Heads

P.H.

To
Congleton

River Dane

0   0.5   Miles   1

START

River Dane

Greens

Manor
Farm

Key to symbols
shown on page 4

Crown Copyright Reserved

29

14. In about ³/₄ mile turn left off the Danebower Hollow track at a metal signpost 'No. 105 Public Footpath via Cumberland Brook to Wildboarclough'.

15. Follow the path across the moor. The path shortly descends to cross a stream then continues on down the moorland with the deep valley of Cumberland Brook on your left and then an old broken wall on the left.

16. Just past an old gatepost on your left cross a broken wall and descend quite steeply to the valley bottom.

17. Walk down the path for a few yards then cross the Brook. Now follow a narrow, rocky but well-established path down the valley, crossing the brook again.

18. On reaching a signpost bear right to cross a stile by a gate following the Wildboarclough route. Continue on down the valley on a wide stony path with Cumberland Brook deep down on your left through the trees.

19. Eventually cross a stile by a gate then in a few yards cross a footbridge, turn right and continue on down the valley.

20. Pass through a gate, cross the road and walk down to a large farm. Turn left to walk through the farmyard then go through a waymarked gate on your left and immediately turn right to follow a wall on your right passing the farmhouse. At the bottom of the field cross a bridge over the river then go through a wall gap and turn left.

21. Follow the minor road for about one mile (passing the turn to Buxton) then turn left through a squeeze stile. (If you wish to call at *The Crag Inn* for refreshments continue along the road for another 50 metres.)

22. Go over the footbridge then in a few metres cross another stream. Walk up the edge of the wood keeping a wall close on your right. At the top of the wood cross a stile. Walk up the field with a stream and wall a few yards to your right.

23. At a waymarked post keep straight on between two broken walls. In about 40 metres cross a footbridge at a wall corner. Continue uphill then on down to cross another footbridge.

24. Walk uphill towards the wood and a waymarked post near the top right hand corner of the rough field. At this post turn right to enter a walled track with the wood on your left.

25. At the top of the track cross the stile and keep straight on passing a woodland on your right and crossing two broken walls. Bear left away from the wood to cross the field and go through a gateway. Keep straight on to cross a stile by another gateway in the field corner.

26. Keep straight on, ignoring a gap on your right, to walk up to the barn. Turn right to walk in front of this barn then go through a gap to follow a wall on your right. At a wall corner continue ahead with a broken wall on your left. Cross a stream and bear right uphill to cross a stile onto the road.

27. Turn left to walk along the road for about ¹/₂ mile. Opposite the road to Wildboarclough turn right at the Footpath sign.

28. Keep straight on up the moorland path shortly bearing left to cross a broken

wall. Now follow the wall on your left until it bends left, here you keep straight on. Shortly the moorland track bends left then right.

29. In about 180 metres, just after passing a small old quarry, cross a waymarked stile by a gate. Keep straight on across the hillside passing two waymarked posts then go through a small gate. Bear off to the right down the steep rocky slope and through a rough grass area. Go through a small gate and bear left.

30. Follow a narrow path through the rough rocky and reedy area to cross a stepped wall stile in the left-hand corner. Continue to follow the narrow path down the valley keeping a wall close on your left.

31. At a waymarked post bear right away from the wall to cross the stream then turn up left to cross a broken wall. Walk diagonally left across a rough field to cross a stile by a field corner and a bar

32. Pass through two gates by the barn on your right. Now walk down a fenced and walled track to pass through another gate and across a minor road. Bear right downhill at a Public Footpath sign.

33. The path winds fairly steeply down through bracken, gorse and grassland. Cross a stile then on down a few steps to the minor road. Turn left for just over 100 metres crossing the Dane river bridge, then turn right over the stile by a gate and retrace your outward journey back to the car park.

CALVER - WALK 9   8 MILES

WHITE EDGE

Curbar Gap - White Edge - Longshaw Estate - Grouse Inn - Froggatt and Curbar Edges

MAP: O.S. Explorer OL. 24. The Peak District White Peak Area

DIRECTIONS: From Baslow take the A623 Stockport to Manchester road. In 1½ miles turn right signposted 'Froggatt 1 Curbar ¼' and in a few metres turn right up Curbar Lane signposted 'Curbar Village'. Follow this uphill for about 1 mile, passing lay-bys on your left. At the top of the hill turn left into the car park (pay and display).

PARKING: Curbar Gap. Grid Ref. S.K. 262747

DESCRIPTION: After a short climb at the start, this is an easy and invigorating walk along the gritstone edges of north east Derbyshire. The views across the Derwent Valley towards Eyam moor, and north towards Carl Wark and Higger Tor are some of the finest in the county. The gritstones were once widely used for making millstones for use in the flour mills; also for cuttings and embankments in the building of the North Midlands Railway and for engine foundations in the lead mines.

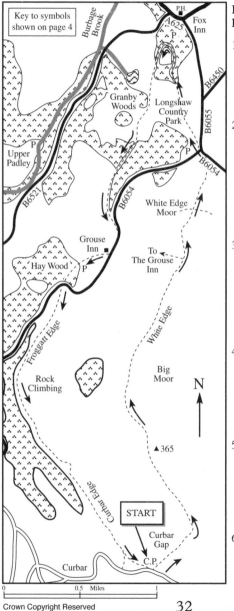

ROUTE INSTRUCTIONS:

1. Leave the car park with the road on your right and cross the car park entrance. Go over a gated stile to enter the 'Eastern Moors Estate'.

2. Continue ahead on a wide track across the moor. Cross a wooden bridge and climb the hill to the wall corner. Turn sharp left at the wall corner and shortly bear right away from the wall up onto the moor.

3. Follow the concessionary path along White Edge for 2 miles ignoring all side paths. Pass through a gap in a wall and keep straight on following the path across the moor signed 'Longshaw'.

4. On reaching a fence and stile (do not cross it) on your left keep straight on. In a few yards you meet a fence and a wall on your left. Follow the line of the fence down to the road.

5. Cross a wall stile. Turn left, cross the road, the grass island and the B6001 and A625 Calver road. Walk to the white gate and go through the small gate to the right.

6. Follow the wide grass track through the National Trust 'Wooden Pole' land. In nearly

half-a-mile pass through another small gate and continue ahead through open woodland.

7. Walk behind Longshaw House and Visitor Centre. Ignore a path off right. Cross the estate drive and go down steps signed 'Footpath No public access on Longshaw Meadow'. Follow the path below the house and then go through two small gates under the yew trees.

8. Follow the estate drive for about 1¼ miles. Go through a small gate by the main white estate gate and turn right down the road to *The Grouse Inn* (an ideal refreshment stop).

9. From the inn turn right for a few steps then cross the stile on your right. Walk down three fields passing through a gateway, across a broken wall and over a stile. Turn left to follow a clear path through the car park, downhill over a stream and up to the road. Turn right, cross the road and go over a stile by a gate.

10. Walk up the wide track with a wall on your right. Enter a birch wood and in nearly ½ mile pass through another kissing gate.

11. Continue along Froggatt and Curbar Edges for 1½ miles keeping to the main path.

12. Come down off the Eastern Moors Estate passing through a gate then continue straight on crossing a small embankment. Follow the path with a wall on your left back to the car park.

CROMFORD - WALK 10   8 MILES

GRATTON DALE - YOULGREAVE

Elton - A5012 - Gratton Dale - Gratton Grange - Bradford Dale - Youlgreave Limestone Way.

MAP: O.S. Explorer OL. 24. The Peak District White Peak Area

DIRECTIONS: Leave the A6 in Cromford to turn left at the traffic lights then in 180 metres turn right onto the A5012 to Buxton and Newhaven. Follow this road for 6 miles along the Via Gellia and passing Grangemill. Take a right turn signed 'Elton'. Follow the minor road, going straight across at the cross roads and ignoring a road off to the right, into Elton. At the T-junction in Elton turn left then immediately right to park by the church.

PARKING: Grid Ref. S.K. 221610.

DESCRIPTION: Gratton Dale and Bradford Dale, through which this walk takes you, are two of the many scenic limestone dales in Derbyshire. Part of the return route is along the well-signposted 'Limestone Way'. From Elton Village the path traverses Elton Common. In the late spring, summer and early autumn *The Elton Tea Rooms* in that village and the *Meadow Cottage Tea Rooms* in Bradford Dale are welcome refreshment stops. Youlgreave is an ancient upland village above Bradford Dale. In June on the Saturday nearest to St. John the Baptist Day, the Youlgreave well-dressing ceremony takes place. The Norman Church has some very fine stained glass by Kempe, William Morris and Burne-Jones. This walk is best done after a period of dry weather.

ROUTE INSTRUCTIONS:

1. At the T-junction turn right. Follow West End Road for about twelve metres and just before the Elton Village Hall turn left up a surfaced path between houses. Go through a stile.
2. Turn right behind the houses and bear left passing 2 waymarked signs. Go through a squeeze stile and follow a path round a small copse of fir trees to another squeeze stile.
3. Keep straight on diagonally across the next field. Go through the squeeze stile by a footpath sign and turn right on a walled track.
4. Turn right along the walled track. Ignore tracks off to the right and left and continue ahead for about 450 metres. Pass through 2 gates and turn left up a roughly surfaced track.
5. Follow the track uphill for near $\frac{1}{2}$ mile passing under power lines. At the top of the hill follow the track round a right-hand bend to pass under another set of power lines.
6. In a few metres, at a footpath post, turn left through a squeeze stile and bear left up the field to go through a wall gap and across a track.
7. Cross the middle of the next field to cross an old wall; continue ahead across the next field passing two large stone troughs on your right. Cross a squeeze stile and continue in more or less the same direction crossing three fields and three stiles.
8. On reaching the road turn right. Walk up the A5012 for about 180 metres. Turn right through a small gate at the 'Gratton Dale and Long Dale' sign.
9. Follow the line of the wall on your left and at the wall corner turn left. In a few yards bear slightly right away from the wall heading for the top of Gratton Dale.
10. Pass through a gateway and follow the path down into Gratton Dale.
11. Pass through a small gate ahead and continue on down the dale.
12. In about $\frac{1}{2}$ mile, opposite a scree slope cross the broken wall on your left. From now on keep to whichever side of the partly demolished wall and

fence that gives better conditions underfoot. However, where a stream emerges, make sure the wall is on your right.

13. Near the end of Gratton Dale (1½ miles) pass through a gate.

14. Continue along the track ahead; if the stream has flooded this track follow a path above it on your left. Go through a gateway near a lime kiln on your left.

15. Keep straight on to the road.

16. Turn left along the road and in about 320 metres fork right uphill to Gratton Grange Farm.

17. Turn left through Gratton Grange farmyard (notice the 1853 barns on your left). Pass through a gate by the garden wall on your left. Cross a small field to pass through another gate ahead.

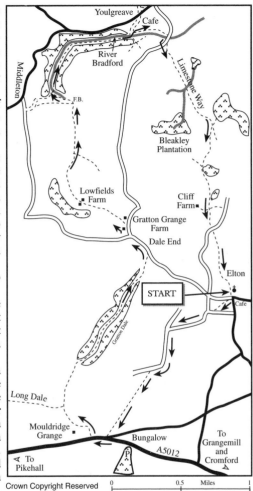

Crown Copyright Reserved

0   0.5   Miles   1

18. Continue straight ahead across the next field and cross a fence stile. Walk up the field keeping a fence on your left until you reach a waymarked stile by a gate on your left. Cross the stile.

19. Turn right and follow the path keeping a fence and a line of trees on your right and passing a waymarked post.

20. At Lowfields Farm cross a waymarked wall stile and walk through the shale yard, then through a gate by a cattle grid.

21. Follow the farm track. Cross a cattle grid and the stream, and in about 30 metres cross a wall stile on your right.
22. Continue ahead keeping the wall on your right. Pass a broken barn on the right and a field wall corner on your left. Keep straight ahead crossing four stiles.
23. Continue across the next field towards the trees. Turn left down a partly stepped path to cross a stone footbridge. Turn left uphill to follow a line of trees on your left.
24. At a waymarked post turn left down metal steps and turn right to follow the path, crossing a concrete footbridge. Join the main Bradford Dale path and turn right.
25. Follow the wide valley path to Youlgreave for about 1 mile.
26. Pass through a metal gate on your left and cross the footbridge. If you wish to stop for refreshments walk up the road to *The Meadow Cottage Tea Rooms*. (Closed Mondays and November-February inclusive) or walk on up to the pubs in Youlgreave.
27. Turn immediately right through a gate signposted 'Limestone Way'. Follow the riverside path and then go through a gated stile onto the road.
28. Follow the road for a short way keeping a wall on your right. Turn right over the bridge and just beyond a barn on your left turn left through a stile signposted 'Public Footpath'.
29. Bear slightly right across the field and cross the stile.
30. Turn half left and follow the two waymarked posts. Go through a stile and bear right up a farm track. Go through a squeeze stile by the right hand gate.
31. Follow the line of the wall on your left. Go through a stile by a gate and bear right across the next large field, following the three way-marked posts.
32. Cross a stream and a stile and continue ahead straight up the field to a fence stile on a bank. Bear left diagonally up the field to a broken wall. Follow the line of this broken wall on your left to an old stone gatepost.
33. Turn left to follow a farm track up and around the gorse hillside. Pass the power line pole and ignore the gates and footpath signs on your left. Pass between two old stone gateposts.
34. Follow the fence and trees on your left. At the end of the trees bear right under the power lines to follow a wall on your right for a few metres. Cross the wall stile ahead.
35. Bear slightly right uphill, following the line of the power cables, to the end of the wood. Pass through a gateway and follow the 'Public Footpath to Elton' sign, keeping a wall and the wood close on your left until you reach another 'Footpath' sign. Turn right across the field. Go through a squeeze stile.
36. Continue straight up the next field to cross a wall stile. Keep straight on across the next small field, cross a farm track and go over a wall stile. Bear slightly left to a fence stile on the horizon.
37. Cross the stile and bear slightly left. Follow a wall on your left downhill for

a short way until you reach a stile. Turn left over the stile and follow a path through a small copse of hawthorn and bramble. Go through a squeeze stile onto the minor road.

38. Cross the road diagonally right to go through a squeeze stile. Keep more or less straight on down the next 4 small fields aiming for Elton at the top of the hill ahead. In the fifth field you will start the uphill climb towards a squeeze stile.

39. Pass through the squeeze stile and continue uphill keeping the field boundary on your left.

40. Turn left at the wall and 'Footpath' sign, then turn right through the gate. Turn right along the village lane, back to the car.

EYAM - WALK 11   9½ **MILES**

Eyam - Highcliffe - Jubilee Plantation - Stoke Ford - Oaks Farm - Abney Moor - Great Hucklow - Grindlow - Foolow - Eyam.

MAPS: O.S. Explorer OL. 24. The Peak District White Peak Area and O.S. Explorer OL. 1. Dark Peak Area

DIRECTIONS: From Calver take the A623 to Stoney Middleton and about ¾ mile from Stoney Middleton turn right up Eyam Dale. In the village of Eyam turn left to follow the road through Eyam, passing the church and Eyam Hall on your right, and car park for Eyam Hall on the left. Turn up Hawkhill road on your right signed 'Car Park'.

PARKING: Grid Ref. S.K. 216767. Car Park - pay and display.

DESCRIPTION: Eyam, meaning an Anglo-Saxon settlement 'Ham' by water 'Ey', is pronounced Eam as in 'steam'. The millstone grit sandstone over the Eyam shales in the hills north of the village ensures that rain water issues from the shale as a series of springs down the 1 mile of the village street. In 1588 stone troughs were built and water conducted to them by pipes; Eyam thus became the first village in the country to have a public water system. This system lasted until the 1920s when piped water was laid on. Eyam is famous as The Plague Village and you can see plaques on many houses telling the story of this terrible time.

The walk starts with a steep climb up Eyam Edge before following the more gentle paths along the western edge of Eyam Moor. From here the route goes down to the delightful picnic spot at Stoke Ford, then climbs steadily up and across Abney Moor from where there are magnificent views. The return route is mainly downhill following well-defined field paths from Great Hucklow.

ROUTE INSTRUCTIONS:

1. From the car park turn right up the road and in 180 metres where the road bends right bear left up a minor 'no through road' which shortly leads into a rough track winding uphill for about ¼ mile.

2. On reaching the road at Highcliffe turn left to walk along the road for nearly ½ mile and on reaching a track up on your right (Sir William Hill road) signed 'Unsuitable for Motor Vehicles', continue to follow the road round a left-hand bend for about 30 metres then turn right down a rough track for just over 275 metres to a crossroads of tracks. Turn right over a ladder stile signed 'Stoke Ford'.

3. Follow a wide path keeping a wall close on your left. In June the rhododendrons of Jubilee Plantation are beautiful. After passing a small low building on your left continue on up to the top corner of a wood and a stone gatepost.

4. Continue ahead along a wide walled grass path for a few metres to cross a stile by a gate then keep straight on following the wall close on your left and going round a right-hand bend. Shortly cross a stile by a gate and turn left.

5. Continue to follow the wall and conifer wood on your left for about 450 metres. On reaching a gate in the corner of the moorland, cross the stile to the left of it and turn right.

6. Follow a wide grass path along the ridge for about ¼ mile, crossing a stile; the path soon veers away from the wall on your right and descends in a curve down into Bretton Clough. Near the bottom the path bends right to join another path where you turn right. Keep the stream down on your left and follow the path down to Stoke Ford. Turn left to cross the bridge.

7. Cross the footbridge and stile over Bretton Brook, turn right to cross another bridge and in a few metres cross a stile on your right signed 'Leadmill, Abney Road ¼ mile' .

8. Continue ahead uphill and through the wood on a path. Eventually, at the boundary of the wood, cross a stile.

9. Walk diagonally right up the field to cross a stile by a gate, cross the road and another stile signed 'Public Footpath to Bradwell, Brough and Shatton 3'.

10. Follow the wide chatter-covered track as it winds uphill. Keep straight on, following the 'Footpath' sign, where the chatter path bears right up to Oaks Farm. Near the top of the hill go over a stile and along a very short, walled path then up to join a farm track.

11. Turn left to follow a wall and wood on your left for about 375 metres. Just past the end of the wood turn right off the farm track and walk up the grass moorland path to a field corner on your left.

12. Turn left ignoring the paths on the right and ahead. Follow the main moorland path as it bears right uphill heading away from the wall; ignore all side paths. In about 450 metres keep straight on at a crossing of wide

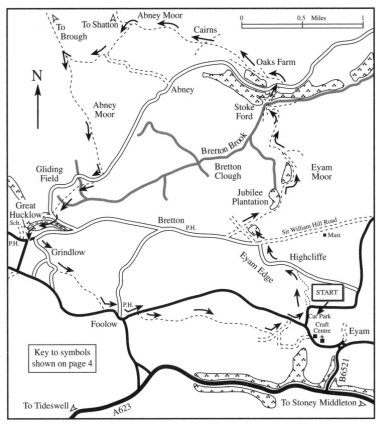

grass paths. In another 230 metres you meet a wall on your left. Follow walls on your left for nearly half a mile.

13. Cross a stile and continue along the moorland path with a fence on your right, then shortly a wall close on your left. Follow this wall as it turns left for about $\frac{1}{3}$ mile along a wide rutted track.

14. At a footpath sign 'Abney' keep straight on following a wide walled track. In just over $\frac{1}{4}$ mile where the track bends right turn left over a stile by a footpath post.

15. Follow the wide moorland path for nearly 1 mile. Cross a stile by a gate and turn right along the road.

39

16. In a few metres veer left across a farm drive and go through a small gate on your left. Cross the middle of the field to the opposite corner and go through another small gate by a farm gate. Follow a path down the steep field, cross a stream and on up the other side following a broken wall on your left and crossing a broken wall.

17. Go through a gated stile, then keep straight on following field paths down into and up out of a small valley, passing a small ruined building and going through three gates. On reaching the road turn left.

18. In about 180 metres, at the far end of a short stretch of railings turn right down to 'The Countryside Commission' notice in Great Hucklow Wood. Follow the signed concessionary path down through the wood. Ignore the small gate and path on your left. Pass the school up on your right. Cross the stile on the right and turn left down to the road junction.

19. At the road junction turn left. (If you want refreshments turn right to *The Queen Anne* pub). In about 140 metres turn right signed 'Grindlow ¼'.

20. Walk through the hamlet of Grindlow and where the road bends sharp right keep straight on by a footpath signpost and a large barn on your right.

21. Follow the walled track with ancient stone slabs for about ⅓ mile. At the end of the track go through a squeeze stile.

22. Continue ahead in a south-easterly direction crossing three fields, four stiles and a farm drive. Turn left along the road.

23. Walk into Foolow passing the village pond on your right and *The Bulls Head* on your left. Walk down the Eyam to Grindleford road for nearly 230 metres. Turn right by a footpath sign and the village sign.

24. Bear left across the field towards a small building. Cross two small squeeze stiles in 25 metres.

25. Now continue in more or less the same easterly direction, crossing many stiles, gates or broken walls, and many small fields (19) for just over 1 mile.

26. Enter a narrow hedged path which leads down to the road. Turn left and walk down to Eyam. At the road junction turn right to walk into the village and in about 275 metres turn left back to the car park.

HARTINGTON - WETTON

The Raikes - Gateham Grange - Wetton - Hopedale - Alstonefield - Gypsy Bank - Dovedale - Wolfscote and Beresford Dales - Hartington.

MAP: O.S. Explorer OL. 24 The Peak District White Peak Area

PARKING: Grid Ref. S.K. 128604. In the centre of Hartington there is a small free car park. A few metres up the B5054 Hulme End-Warslow road is a pay and display car park.

DIRECTIONS: From Ashbourne take the A515 to Buxton. In ten miles turn left to Hartington two miles.

DESCRIPTION: The Derbyshire village of Hartington attracts many visitors, having a Stilton cheese factory and shop, a sheepskin shop and craft and book shops, as well as a number of inns and teashops. From Hartington the first part of the walk is across the undulating fields of North Staffordshire and through the delightful villages of Wetton and Alstonefield where you may visit an interesting Art Gallery. *The Royal Oak* (closed Wednesdays), *The Watts Russell* in Hope and *The George* in Alstonefield provide refreshment stops. The return route follows the lovely river Dove.

ROUTE INSTRUCTIONS:

1. From the free car park in Hartington walk past *The Charles Cotton Hotel* on your right up the B5054 Warslow road. In a few metres just before the Ceramic Works and Shop on your left, turn right at the end of a wall in front of a row of stone houses.
2. Follow the wall and house wall to pass through a stone squeeze stile.
3. Walk along a very narrow path between buildings, then between a fence and a wall. Pass through a gate and continue to follow the path, to go over a stile.
4. Follow the line of the wall close on your left. Cross a wall stile.
5. Keep straight on crossing the next five fields and five stiles maintaining a south-westerly direction. In the fourth and fifth fields aim for a cottage and the road.
6. After a fifth stile turn left then immediately right onto the B5054. Follow the road uphill, crossing into Staffordshire, for about 500 metres, passing Raikes Farm on your right and Lower Hurst Farm entrance on your left.

7. Just past the 'Little Raikes Footpath' sign and the cottage turn left signposted 'Public Footpath,' cross the stile and descend the field keeping a wall and fence on your left.

8. Cross a stile and footbridge, walk up the field ahead. Cross another stile.

9. Bear right up the field following the right-hand 'Footpath' sign. Pass above the farm. Cross a waymarked fence and wall stile.

10. Continue ahead to cross another wall stile by a water trough. Bear slightly left passing a tennis court and having a fence on your left.

11. Cross a stile and walk straight ahead up the shallow field valley, keeping trees on your left and the steep bank on your right.

12. Cross a squeeze stile. Bear slightly right to walk up the next field crossing a stile and continuing ahead to cross another stile.

13. Turn left along the road. Go straight on at the crossroads following the sign, Wetton 2^1/$_4$, Alstonefield 2^1/$_2$. In about 450 metres turn left through a gated stile at the 'Footpath' sign by a gate.

14. Continue ahead keeping the fence and wood close on your right. Go through a small gate. Follow the fence for a short way then at its corner keep straight on to a waymarked post and cross a footbridge.

15. Follow the hawthorn trees on your left then bear right to cross a fence stile. Bear right up the next field.

16. Cross a fence stile and walk downhill to cross another fence stile and a stream. Continue ahead up the shallow field valley and near the top turn left across a marshy area.

17. Cross a fence stile. Walk up the field with a wall on your left for a short way. At the field corner bear slightly left away from the wall.

18. Pass a barn a little way off on your left. Keep straight on crossing the undulating field in the direction of road signs to be seen on the horizon. (Cross the stream at the best place you can find.) Walk up the steep field towards a gate and cross a waymarked stile just short of the gate.

19. Turn right up the road. At the crossroads keep straight on signposted 'Wetton 1^1/$_4$'. In about 275 metres where the road bends left, turn right through a stile signed 'Public Footpath'.

20. Continue ahead towards Wetton Hill, pass through a stile onto National Trust land and turn left heading for a wall corner.

21. Follow the wall close on your left and cross the first stile on your left. Turn right to cross the field to another squeeze and wooden stile.

22. Continue straight ahead crossing 7 fields and 7 stiles. Pass above a small copse in the seventh field.

23. Turn sharp right across the top of a narrow field and go over a wall stile. Turn left to follow a wall on your left and cross another stile by a gate. Continue ahead to cross another stile leading onto a lane. Turn left down the lane.

24. At the road junction turn left and walk through Wetton passing *Ye Olde*

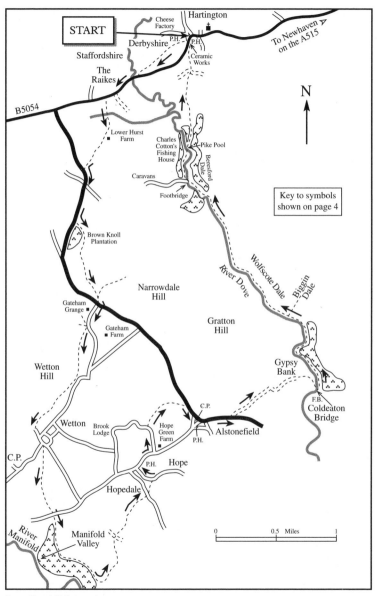

START

Hartington

Cheese Factory

P.H.

Derbyshire

P.H.

Ceramic Works

To Newhaven on the A515

Staffordshire

The Raikes

B5054

N

Lower Hurst Farm

Charles Cotton's Fishing House

Pike Pool

Beresford Dale

Caravans

Footbridge

Key to symbols shown on page 4

Brown Knoll Plantation

Wolfscote Dale

River Dove

Biggin Dale

Narrowdale Hill

Gateham Grange

Gratton Hill

Gateham Farm

Wetton Hill

Gypsy Bank

F.B.
Coldeaton Bridge

Wetton

Brook Lodge

Hope Green Farm

C.P.

P.H.

Alstonefield

C.P.

P.H.

Hope

Hopedale

0   0.5   Miles   1

River Manifold

Manifold Valley

Royal Oak inn on your right.

25. At the next road junction turn right signposted 'Grindon 2¹/₂ (Manifold Valley)' and 'Toilets' and almost immediately left again up a short grass path to go through a squeeze stile signposted 'Footpath'.

26. Walk diagonally right across a narrow field to cross a stile.

27. Continue diagonally slightly left across the next three fields and stiles.

28. Head up the next field towards a barn on the skyline. About 25 metres to the left of the barn cross a wall stile and continue down the field with a wall on your right.

29. Cross a stile, cross the lane and the stile opposite. Cross the next field to a squeeze stile.

30. Turn right and where the wall on your left turns left keep straight on to cross a stile in the opposite wall.

31. Continue uphill bearing slightly left to keep walls and fences up on your left.

32. Contour the hillside for about half a mile crossing two broken walls (notice the Manifold Valley down on your right).

33. Go through a small gate and walk up the hill with the wall on your left to cross a stile by a farm gate.

34. Bear slightly left on a wide grass path heading for a tall signpost.

35. At the signpost follow the 'Public Footpath to Hope Dale' direction, crossing two squeeze stiles and a farm track.

36. Cross the next field diagonally left to go through a squeeze stile. Then cross five fields and four stiles keeping a wall close on your left for the first three and a half fields (in the fourth field bear left).

37. Go through a small gate and continue ahead with a wall now on your right. At the bottom of the field cross a stile.

38. Cross a minor road and a stile. Walk down into the valley bottom and turn left. Cross the stile and turn left along the road.

39. Walk through Hopedale village, passing the *Watts Russell* inn on your right and on up the hill ignoring the road to Ilam on your left.

40. Take the first left turn and pass Hope Green Farm. In nearly 375 metres turn right at the second stile on your right; this is opposite a footpath post on your left.

41. Walk up the field keeping the wall on your left, cross a stile and continue ahead with the wall now on your right to cross 2 fields and 1 gated stile.

42. Cross a stile by a gate and enter a walled track which leads into Alstonefield. At the T-junction turn right.

43. Walk through the village following the Ashbourne signs, passing a car park sign and a car park on your right; round a left-hand bend and passing the side of *The George* inn and the village green on your right. Follow the Lode Mill and Ashbourne road out of the village.

44. Turn left at the <u>second</u> 'Public Footpath' and Youth Hostel signs and walk along a walled track passing barns.

45. Follow the track, which has a sharp right and left-hand bend, down to the top of 'Gypsy Bank'. Cross the stile.
46. Bear right down the steep hillside to cross Coldeaton Bridge. Turn left.
47. Follow the river Dove for two and a half miles. Along this beautiful stretch of the route, which takes you through Wolfscote Dale and Beresford Dale, you will cross six stiles and two bridges (ignoring the first two bridges) and see the magnificent cliffs at the entrance to Biggin Dale and Drabber Tor in Wolfscote Dale; also the tall limestone pillar in the Pike Pool by the second bridge in Beresford Dale. By this pool is the wall of Charles Cotton's fishing house from which he and Izaak Walton went fishing.
48. In a short distance after crossing the Dove over the second bridge, start to climb up away from the river. Go through a gated stile and keep straight on up the field path to follow the line of an old wall. Descend the field and pass through a stile by a gate.
49. Bear right to walk up the field, go through a broken wall and bear right again uphill to pass waymarked posts. Cross two gated stiles on either side of a rough track. Follow the waymarked and clearly-defined path to Hartington.
50. Pass through a small metal gate and down steps by the toilets. Cross the forecourt of the Ceramic Works to join the B5054. Turn right into the village centre car park or left to the pay and display car park.

HATHERSAGE - WALK 13   12 OR 9 MILES

STANAGE EDGE

Stanage Edge - Stanedge Pole - Redmires Reservoirs - Surrey Farm - Crawshaw Lodge - Crawshaw Farm - Wet Shaw Lane - Stake Hill Road - Moscar - Stanage Edge.

MAP: O.S. Explorer OL. 1. The Peak District Dark Peak Area

DIRECTIONS: From Hathersage take the A6178 Hope road. Just after passing *The George Hotel* turn right up Jaggers Lane in just over 275 metres, turn right up Coggers Lane. Where the road forks take the left fork, and continue to the car park at Dennis Knoll. Grid ref. SK.228843.

DESCRIPTION: This walk starts by following a wide causeway, possibly of Roman origin, up onto Stanage Edge then via The Long Causeway to the Yorkshire/Derbyshire boundary at Stanedge Pole before descending to the

Redmires Reservoirs. From here the route follows undulating moorland paths before reaching the A57 and climbing up to a ridge at Crawshaw Lodge. Here you have a choice of either turning west along a minor road for just over 1 mile or continuing northwards and then southwards over another moor and farmland area before rejoining the shorter route at Moscar. The return path along Stanage Edge is very enjoyable and impressive.

ROUTE INSTRUCTIONS:

1. Leave the car park and follow the wide track as it gradually climbs the hillside up onto Stanage Edge (about $^1/_2$ mile).
2. On reaching a stile on your right keep straight on to follow the Long Causeway uphill with a fence on your left and a broken wall on your right.
3. As you leave the wall the causeway bends left and continues to climb gently up to Stanedge Pole on the horizon.
4. At the Pole continue along the Causeway towards the Redmires Reservoirs in the distance. You will pass through one gate.
5. At the reservoirs follow the causeway round to the left to join a surfaced road which you follow for nearly $^1/_2$ mile. Just beyond the car park on your left turn left through a swing gate and walk up a wide woodland track then on up the moorland path. This path shortly descends to cross a valley and a stile before ascending the moorland.
6. Continue on up the moorland keeping a wall on your right. At the wall corner keep straight on and in about 180 metres you follow a broken wall on your left.
7. Cross the small bridge over the conduit and go over the stile ahead. Follow the path down the moorland keeping a wall on your left. Notice the Head Stone on your left. At a waymarked post keep straight on down the moorland path towards the main road.
8. At the bottom of the moorland cross the footbridge and go through the stile ahead. Bear right up the field to cross a wall stile by a gate.
9. Cross the main A57 and turn right and in about 30 metres go over a wooden stile on your left signposted 'Public Footpath'. Walk up the field passing Surrey Farm on your left and go through a squeeze stile. Keep straight on up the middle of the next field to cross a wall stile by another 'Footpath' sign and continue ahead to follow a path up through the reeds and scrubland. Cross a stile onto the minor road at Crawshaw Lodge. (If you wish to do the 9 mile walk turn left to follow the road for just over 1 mile. Where the road bends round to the left leave it and keep straight on along a sandy track. In about 230 metres go through a gate and continue in the same direction for another 230 metres down to join the longer route coming in on the right. Now follow route instruction no.17.)
10. Turn right for just over 100 metres then turn very sharp left to walk through the gateway of Crawshaw Lodge. Follow the drive behind the

46

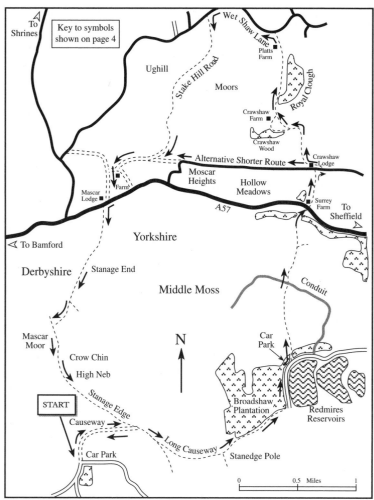

Lodge then go over a stile by a gate. Keep straight on following the farm drive uphill, across and round the moorland for about ½ mile.

11. Just before Crawshaw Farm turn right off the farm drive and go over a wall stile by a gate and a footpath sign on your right. Walk down to the middle of the field, pass the farmhouse on your left then cross a stile by a gate.

12. Bear right down the farm drive and follow it for about ³/₄ of a mile. At the road junction turn left.

13. Follow Wet Shaw Lane for about ¹/₂ mile. Pass a wood and footpath on your right, and in 100 metres turn left through a gate.

14. Walk up a wide fenced and walled track for 230 metres, go through a gate and keep straight on up the hill. At the top of the field follow a walled track uphill. In nearly ¹/₂ mile go through a gate onto the moorland.

15. Keep straight on and in a few yards the path becomes a broken walled track again. This is the ancient Stake Hill Road. In about ¹/₂ mile go through a gate and keep straight on down with a broken wall on your right.

16. In about 230 metres join a path coming in on the left (the shorter route).

17. Now keep straight on along a wide walled rough track, passing through a gate, then walk behind a farm and go through two gateways. At a wall ahead turn left off the track to pass the boundary stone on your right. Walk down a wide walled grass track to the A57 passing Moscar Lodge on your right.

18. Cross the A57, turn right and in a few metres turn left at the 'Footpath' sign, then go over a stile onto the moors.

19. Follow the moorland path uphill for about ³/₄ mile to the outcrops of rocks and stretches of wall at Stanage Edge. Ignore a path up to your left and keep straight on. Shortly the path bends right downhill away from the high gritstone edge. *This stretch can be very boggy.* In a few metres at a T-junction of paths turn left and continue on a more definite path with the Edge up on your left.

20. In about another ¹/₂ mile you will pass below the impressive Crow Chin rocks. The views of Win Hill and the Kinder Plateau beyond are very commanding. As you walk below High Neb notice the many millstones on the heather slopes.

21 Continue along the main path. Ignore all paths off left and right. Eventually you will reach a ladder stile. Cross this and turn left to join the causeway. Turn right.

22. Retrace your outward route back to the car park.

HATHERSAGE - WALK 14   9¹/₂ MILES

Leadmill - Mount Pleasant - Callow Wood - Offerton - Shatton Lane - Brough Lane - Brough - Townfield Lane - Derwent Valley - Stepping Stones - Hathersage

MAP: O.S. Explorer OL. 1 The Peak District Dark Peak Area

DIRECTIONS AND CAR PARK: From the Hope to Hathersage road turn onto the B6001 opposite *The George Hotel* in Hathersage. Turn left and the car park is on your left. Grid Ref. SK. 232814.

DESCRIPTION: This is a very pleasant walk especially in the late Spring through the beautiful bluebell woods of Callow, then along clear bridleways and lanes over the bracing Offerton and Shatton Moors. If you wish to take refreshments at *The Travellers Rest* follow the diversion described under instruction No. 14 of the route. The return path follows the lovely Derwent river. After prolonged heavy rain, some of the stepping stones may be covered. If this is so, proceed along the riverside path to instruction No. 2 where you left the riverside path on your outward route. Now retrace your steps back to the car park.

ROUTE INSTRUCTIONS:

1. From the car park main entrance turn right down the road to the B6001, turn left and in a few metres turn right down Dore Lane. Pass under the railway bridge. On reaching the entrance to Nether Hall at the bend in the road turn left over a stile by a gate. Follow the farm drive, then a path, keeping a fence on your right and crossing three stiles.
2. Turn right along the B6001, go over the Derwent then immediately turn right through the wall and over a stile. Follow the riverside path for about 230 metres. By a stile turn away from the river.
3. Follow a line of old posts across the field and up a short steep path through a small wood, at the top of which cross a wall stile. Turn right and follow the path uphill keeping the wall fence and wood on your right and crossing one stile.
4. At the end of the wall and fence keep straight on uphill to cross a stile onto a minor road. Turn sharp right down a farm drive signed 'Broadhay Farm'. In about 230 metres, turn left through a gate at a Footpath sign.
5. Walk up the field and under the power lines, turn left to follow the power lines for a few metres before veering away from them up onto a banked grass track which leads to a stile by a gate. Cross this and enter Callow Wood.

6. Follow the wide woodland path and in nearly 140 metres bear right uphill off the main track heading for a wall at the edge of the wood. Eventually pass through a small gate to leave the wood.

7. Bear slightly left up the field to go through a stile and then a small gate. Walk up the farm drive for about 20 metres. Go through a gateway and turn right. Walk behind Callow Farm.

8. Follow the well-defined path up through the bracken crossing a stile, a small valley, then about 375 metres further on another stile.

9. Turn right along the minor road, in about 320 metres pass Offerton Hall on your right and at a sharp right-hand bend keep straight on to cross the right-hand stile by an old gate signed 'Public Bridleway'.

10. Follow this bridleway up Offerton Moor for just over $^3/_4$ mile. Cross a ladder stile and turn left up a minor road for a few metres to go through a gate across the road onto Shatton Lane.

11. Follow this lane across Shatton Moor for about one mile passing a mast and going through one gate. At the end of the lane pass through old stone gateposts and turn left to follow a rutted track round the hill for a short way. On reaching a signpost 'Stoke Ford' turn right.

12. Follow the rutted track keeping a wall close on your left. Pass a road on your left signed 'Abney' and keep straight on along a wide stony track (this short stretch is also included in Walk 11).

13. Follow the main track round to the right (Brough Lane). Follow this stony track for just over $1^1/_2$ miles, passing through one gate. Towards the end of this track it becomes a surfaced road which you follow downhill.

14. At a sharp left-hand bend turn right. *If you wish to stop for refreshments keep on down the road to Brough where you turn right, go over the bridge and on up to the A625 to* The Traveller's Rest. *Retrace your steps to follow the route. This diversion will add about $^1/_2$ mile onto the walk.*

15. Follow a track which crosses two stiles by gates then continues ahead up a sunken section. Pass through a gate to follow the track round a large field with a wall then a hedge on your right.

16. Pass through a gate and turn left to follow Townfield Lane for about 75 metres, then fork right on to a wide track. Follow this track, and ignoring the point where it joins Townfield Lane, keep straight on at the footpath sign to follow the path which goes behind stone and corrugated buildings. Go through a small gate and over a stile. Follow the field boundary on your left to go through another gate and down steps. Cross the lane to go up steps and over a stile.

17. Keep straight on crossing three fields and three stiles. Walk down the road for a few metres then turn left at the T-junction. In about 140 metres, just before a bridge and the main road, turn right over a stile signed 'Public Footpath Leadmill'.

18. Follow a well-defined path, cross a footbridge then continue along

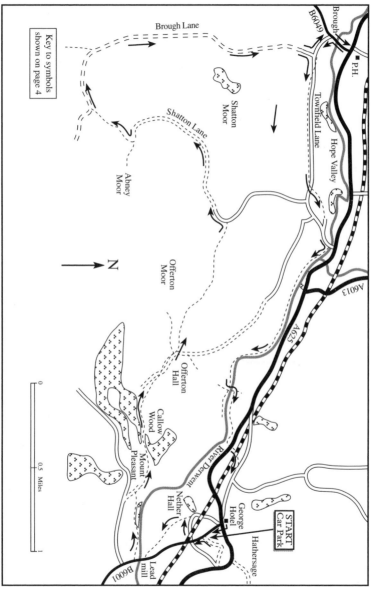

51

the undulating riverside path for just over one mile. You will cross 6 stiles, two bridges, and gates or gateways depending on the time of the year. After the sixth stile bear left keeping to the riverside path.

19. On reaching a footpath post turn left to cross the stepping stones over the River Derwent. Climb the steps and cross a stile. Continue to follow the river, now on your right, for nearly $^1/_4$ mile, crossing one stile.

20. Bear left away from the river up to a small gate in the field corner. Pass through this gate, cross the A625, go over a stile then up a narrow field to go over a ladder stile. Cross the railway line then over another ladder stile.

21. Walk diagonally right up the next field to go through a small gate by a farm gate in the field corner. Turn right and follow Jagger's Lane down to the A625.

22. Turn left to pass *The George Hotel* on your left. Just before the National Westminster Bank turn right and walk up the church drive, then along a short fenced path to the car park.

LEEK - WALK 15 $8^1/_2$ MILES

THE ROACHES

Five Clouds - Roche Grange - Turner's Pool - Swythamley Hall - Danebridge - The Roaches

MAP: O.S. Explorer OL. 24 The Peak District White Peak Area

DIRECTIONS: From Leek take the A53 to Buxton. In just over 3 miles turn left to Upper Hulme. Or take the A53 from Buxton and in $8^1/_2$ miles turn right to Upper Hulme. Follow the narrow winding road through the village. Nearly 1 mile past the village there are small lay-by car parks below 'Five Clouds'. Parking is restricted to the marked areas. At the weekends and on bank holidays from mid-spring to mid-autumn 'Park and Ride' operates from the The Tittesworth reservoir car park. At any other time it is advisable to arrive early.

PARKING: Grid ref. S.K.004621. Grid ref. for reservoir car park S.J.994602

DESCRIPTION: This Peak District walk, in an area dominated by rocky fringes, follows interesting paths through farmland, along country lanes, across open moorland and along gritstone edges. There are magnificent views over the Staffordshire countryside. The Roaches, like the eastern Edges of Froggatt and Stanage, are of millstone grit rock. Wind erosion is dramatically evident on many of the huge rock outcrops of the Roaches and the Five Clouds. The latter are seen as five rock bluffs standing out from the heather below the Roaches Edge. For further information on Millstone Grit Edges, read the article in the March 1995 issue of *Derbyshire Life and Countryside*.

It is advisable to follow this walk in dry weather as the farmlands between 5 and 10 on the route directions can be boggy. If you wish to have a pub meal, follow the road into Danebridge and up towards Wincle, as shown on the sketch map. Rejoin the walk route at Paddock Farm.

ROUTE INSTRUCTIONS:

1. With the parking bay on your right continue along the minor road for 1 mile. Turn left following the 'Leek, Meerbrook' sign.
2. At the bottom of the hill pass Roche Grange Farm, and where the road bends left turn right along the Brownsett Farm track to cross a stile by a gate and a cattle grid.
3. Almost immediately turn left away from the track and walk towards an old standing stone, then bear right to follow a wide grass path (at first not easily recognisable). This path leads you round the hill towards old stone gate-posts (not the gateposts at the bottom of the field).
4. Continue ahead to cross a stile then walk downhill to a stone barn, by a waymarked footpath post. Continue ahead through a gateway.
5. Keep the barn and then the line of an old fence close on your left. Cross a stile in the field corner.
6. Cross a small narrow stream (no bridge) turn sharp left, cross a fence stile.
7. Bear right diagonally across the field with the metal barns of Meadow Farm on your left. At the field corner pass through a small gate to enter a rough farm track and turn right to follow this track.
8. In a short distance the track enters a field. Turn left to follow an old fence and a line of trees on your left. At the field corner cross a gated footbridge.
9. Cross the middle of the next field bearing down diagonally left to pass through a gateway.
10. Continue ahead up the rough field to pass above a clump of trees and a holly bush on your left. At the field corner cross a stile by a waymarked post.
11. Continue ahead with the wood on your left. Cross a stile by a gate and follow the 'Turner's Pool' footpath keeping the wood on your left. Cross another stile. Pass Turner's Pool on your left. This is a popular area for fishermen.
12. On reaching the lane continue straight on following the lane round a right-hand bend to pass through a way-marked gate.

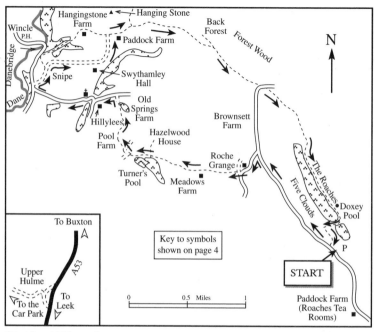

13. Pass a stone barn on your left, turn right and in 20 metres bear left over a stile signed 'Please'. Follow the narrow wooden stepped path round Pool Farm. Turn right at the bottom of the steps and walk through open woodland to cross a waymarked stile.

14. Bear right up the field, keeping a rough area to your left, pass through a line of trees and head up the field to cross a fence stile.

15. Bear slightly right towards the opposite fence walking below the conifer wood. Cross a fence stile by a gate.

16. Bear right up the field towards Old Springs Farm. Cross a stile by a 'Public Footpath' post. Turn left and walk through the farmyard and then left again at the footpath post to cross a cattle grid.

17. Turn left along the minor road passing Hillylees Farm and turn right at the T-junction. Follow this road for ¹/₂ mile passing Swythamley Hall, Park and Church on your right.

18. Just after a road junction on your left turn sharp right signed 'Hanging Stone Farm' and 'Paddock Farm'. In 30 metres turn left signposted 'Public Footpath Back Forest 1¹/₂ Gradbach 2¹/₂ ' (*or if you wish to visit*

54

Danebridge continue along the minor road after the road junction on your left. Rejoin the route at instruction 20).

19. Follow the 'Private Road' for 1 mile, ignoring a stile on your left; crossing a stile by a cattle grid; <u>passing</u> the private farm road to Hanging Stone Farm on your left; and following the lane round a left-hand bend, to Paddock Farm below the Hanging Stone. (*At this point you may wish to climb up to the Hanging Stone for a picnic.*)

20. Pass the entrance to Paddock Farm on your right and continue uphill bearing slightly right to the signpost 'Gradbach'. Walk behind Paddock Farm. Cross a stile by a gate onto open moorland.

21. Follow the 'Roach End' path ahead ignoring the path up to the left. Keep a wall on your right to follow the path, crossing one stile, for about $^3/_4$ mile.

22. Join the ridge path, turn right, keeping a wall close on your right.

23. Cross two stiles and a minor road. Climb the stepped path opposite onto The Roaches Estate. Keep to the main edge path all the way for about $1^1/_2$ miles. Nearing the end of the path you pass Doxy Pool and in about another 5 minutes walking you will have a rough wall on your right.

24. At the end of the wall by a short length of fencing on your left turn right down a steep gully. At a waymarked crossroads of paths, carry straight on down a narrow path. Pass through an open conifer wood then through a gateway.

25. Follow the path across rough moorland, then down a sunken path to steps, at the bottom of which, turn left.

26. Follow this path down to the road and back to your car.

The Roaches Tea Rooms near Upper Hulme provide a welcome tea stop.

TIDESWELL - WALK 16   8$^1/_2$ MILES

WYE VALLEY

Miller's Dale - Tideswell Dale - Tideswell - Peter Dale - Wormhill - Wye Valley - Monsal Trail

MAP: O.S. Outdoor Leisure 24 The Peak District White Peak Area

DIRECTIONS: From Tideswell take the B6049. After passing through Miller's Dale and under the Monsal Trail bridge turn sharp right signed 'Wormhill'. In about 230 metres turn left into the Pay & Display car park. Grid ref. S.K. 138 733.

DESCRIPTION: The walk starts with a leisurely stroll through Miller's Dale then along a pleasant riverside minor road before a gentle climb up Tideswell Dale. The large parish church of St. John the Baptist in Tideswell - known as The Cathedral of the Peak - stands on the site of an 11th century chapelry recorded in Domesday Book. Lead mining, quarrying, agriculture, velvet-cutting mills and cotton and silk weaving occupied the past inhabitants of this small market town. Tideswell was granted a charter in 1250. Markets are still held twice a year but no longer for cattle; instead local crafts and produce are sold including the oatcakes once cooked on the old-fashioned bakestone. It is believed that the site has been occupied since Celtic times when a chieftain by the name of Tiddy owned the well nearby.

From Tideswell you will follow field paths to join the Limestone Way which you follow up Peter Dale to Dale Head before returning south to Wormhill. From here you descend to the Wye Valley before climbing up to the Monsall Trail.

ROUTE INSTRUCTIONS:

1. Leave the car park by the main entrance and turn right down the road passing under the Monsal Trail and crossing the bridge over the Wye. Turn left along the B6049 signed 'Tideswell Litton Mill'.
2. Walk through the interesting hamlet of Miller's Dale passing the Craft and Education Centres. About 140 metres after passing under the Monsal Trail (which you will have followed in walk no. 2) fork right onto the minor road to 'Litton Mill only'.
3. Follow this quiet and pretty riverside road for nearly 1 mile to just before the hamlet of Litton Mill.
4. Just past the National Trust property of Ravenstor and the 'No Public Parking beyond this point' notice, turn very sharp left at a waymarked post. Follow a wide woodland path as it gradually climbs the very gentle slope up Tideswell Dale (total length is just over 1 mile). About halfway up you will cross either the first or second bridge and turn left to follow a surfaced path, then further on you walk through a car park and picnic area. At the end of the car park keep straight on to follow a short path with tall beech trees on your left.
5. On reaching the road turn right through a small gate. Follow a path with a wall and the road on your left.
6. On reaching a fence in front of you go through a small gate on your left then cross the B6049 and turn right. Walk up the road into Tideswell.
7. Just past the 30mph sign and Richard Lane and above the bus shelter,

turn left through a wide wall gap and walk up through the trees on a stepped path. Pass through a stile. Turn right along the road for about 230 metres and opposite a post-box on a street lamp pole turn left up the narrow Brockley Lane. (*If you want to stop for refreshments continue on along the road into the village centre where there are pubs and cafes.*)

8. At the top of Brockley Lane turn right for a few metres and just past Primrose Lane, which is on your right, turn left through a stile by a gate.

9. Walk up a short wide walled track to enter a field. Keep straight on with the walls on your right to cross 10 fields, 11 stiles and 1 lane. In the eighth, ninth and tenth fields you will bear slightly left.

10. After crossing a very narrow field, go through a gateway signed 'Public Footpath' and keep straight on down a large field. Pass a dew pond on your left then cross a stile at a field corner.

11. Walk up the next field following a wall on the right. Cross a stile and turn right up a track for 230 metres; at the road junction turn left to follow the Limestone Way downhill.

12. In just under $\frac{1}{2}$ mile, at the bottom of the hill turn right to enter Monks Dale still following the Limestone Way. This soon becomes Peter Dale.

13. Walk up the very gentle sloping Peter Dale for about 1 mile. (In late spring there is a great variety of flowers in this open limestone dale.)

14. At Dale Head cross a high wall stile and turn left up the minor road for about 75 metres then turn left over a stile signed 'Public Footpath'. Walk up an old walled track for about 180 metres then pass through a waymarked gateway into a field.

15. Keep straight on with a wall on your left, shortly the path veers away from the wall to cross the top of a small valley, then on up to cross a stile to the right of a gate.

16. Walk up the next field keeping a wall close on your left. Cross a high walled stile by a gate in the field corner. Follow a farm track with a wall now on your right and shortly passing through a gate.

17. Bear left up the hill to the telegraph pole and a small copse, cross the stile by the telegraph pole. Bear left to cross a stile by a water trough. Continue ahead with a wall on your left to cross two fields and two stiles.

18. Almost immediately after the second stile go through a gate on your left and turn right, to cross two small fields and two stiles and up a large field keeping a wall close on your right all the way.

19. Cross a stile at the field corner and turn right up the road. In about 275 metres at the road junction turn left and walk down the footpath towards Wormhill.

20. In 180 metres turn left at the 'no through road' sign. Walk down the road and round the right-hand bend then follow the waymarked sign

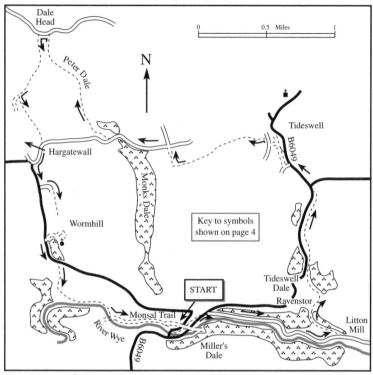

passing the end of a cottage on your left (RTG 1991). Go through a gate.

21. Follow the walls mainly on your left then on your right to cross 7 fields 8 stiles and 1 lane.

22. Follow the short track which leads to the road past the church.

23. Walk up to the T-junction and turn left. Pass Wellhead Farm on your right. In about 375 metres, at the derestriction sign, bear right down a gravel track which bends right, past a cottage on the left, then on down a narrow walled path and through the woods.

24. Ignore a path off to the right and keep to the main path as it contours round the hillside before descending gradually down a rocky path.

25. On reaching the river Wye at a footbridge turn left to follow the Monsal Trail.

26. At the viaduct turn left up a flight of steps signed 'Monsal Trail'. Turn left to follow the trail back to the car park.

WINSTER - WALK 17   7¹/₂ MILES

Winster - Limestone Way - Brumlea Farm - Moor Lane - Green Lane - Grangemill - Aldwark - Green Low - Winster.

MAP: O.S. Explorer OL. 24. The Peak District White Peak Area.

DIRECTIONS: From the centre of Winster, with 'Winster Market House National Trust Information Centre' on your left, drive through the village then turn left up West Bank. In nearly ¹/₂ mile near the top of the hill and before you join the B5056 turn left into a small 'Parking' area. Grid Ref. S.K.238602.

DESCRIPTION: The area covered by this walk is in the south-eastern corner of the Peak Park and is not so frequently walked, especially the paths in the Brumlea Farm to Bottom Leys Farm area.

Winster is in the centre of a big lead-mining area as you will see when you cross the hummocky fields. It is an ancient market town with some interesting late 17th century houses including the Market Hall.

The Holly Bush Inn at Grangemill and *The Miners Standard* near Winster are suitable refreshment stops.

ROUTE INSTRUCTIONS:

1. From the small parking area, turn left up the road for a few yards to join the B5056 and keep straight on for about 80 metres. Turn left onto the Limestone Way.
2. Follow the walled track for just over ¹/₂ mile.
3. Cross a stile by a gate and in a few metres pass through a gateway on your left then bear right downhill passing 2 standing stones and an old wall on your left and passing three trees on your right. Head for a waymarked stile. The Lunter Rocks are way up to your right.
4. Cross the stile following the line of an old wall and a wood on your right. Pass through a gated squeeze stile in the field corner. Keep straight on and in about 75 metres cross a stile on your right and turn left uphill to go through another squeeze stile.
5. Keep straight on following a wall on your left and crossing two broken walls and two fields. After the second broken wall bear right up the field, go through a squeeze stile, cross the corner of the next field and through another stile.
6. Bear very slightly right across the next 2 fields. Cross a stile and a farm track and keep straight on to cross another stile. Bear right passing under power lines and aiming for the field corner and the footpath sign. Cross the stile.

Turn left along the road for about 100 metres. Turn right over a stile.

7. Walk diagonally up the field, pass through a gap then cross the corner of the next field to go through another stile. Follow the path across the middle of the next hummocky field. Cross a stile and keep straight on towards an old barn crossing a broken wall and two fields and passing the barn on your left.

8. Cross a stile in the field corner turn left then right onto a gravel track (Blakelow Lane). In about 30 metres turn left through a stile then bear slightly right across the next field and through one squeeze stile to join an old wall on your right.

9. Go through a squeeze stile and cross the end of a very narrow field to go through another stile by a gateway. Bear left across another two small fields and through two stiles. Now walk down the next larger field keeping a wall on your left.

10. Cross through a stile by a footpath sign and turn left along an old walled track (Moorlands Lane). In about 75 metres turn right off the track and through a stile.

11. Walk down the next two fields and over one stile keeping a wall on your left. About 50 metres down the second field turn left through a broken wall and immediately right to follow an old walled gated grass track. In just over 275 metres cross a stile by a 'Footpath' sign on your right.

12. Bear left across the field and pass through a stile in the bushes. Walk down the next field, cross a stile by a wall corner and keep straight on passing Brumlea Farm on your left. Cross a stile by a 'Footpath' post.

13. Turn right up the farm track (Moor Lane). In about 100 metres turn left up and through a stile. Bear right up the middle of the next field.

14. Continue in the same direction crossing 2 fields. In the corner of the second field enter a very short walled track to go through a waymarked stile. Bear right down and across the slope of the field to go through a stile in the hawthorn hedge. Keep straight on across the slope passing more hawthorn bushes on your right.

15. Cross a stile under the ash tree.

16. Keep straight on for about 40 metres then turn left downhill to cross a small riverless valley then up to an old small stone building on your left. At the waymarked post on your right bear right uphill.

17. Pass through a small wooded area. Soon you will have a wall on your right as you climb the hill. Just before a wall across the path, turn right through a wall gap by an ash tree and a waymarked post. Turn left up a very narrow strip field.

18. At the top of the field turn right to follow a rough walled track for about 20 metres then turn left by a 'Footpath' sign.

19. Cross the next field passing Bottom Leys Farm on your right. Cross the stile and bear right across the field corner to cross another stile. Keep straight on to a waymarked post ahead.

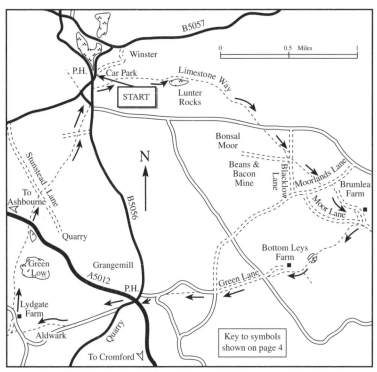

20. Cross a broken wall then walk through a hummocky rough field towards a waymarked post. Keeping the drive and fence on your right walk up the field to cross a stile in the corner.

21. Cross the minor road diagonally right to enter Green Lane which you follow for nearly ¹/₂ mile. At a crossroads keep straight on to follow a surfaced road downhill.

22. In about 180 metres turn left through a gated stile. Continue downhill in more or less the same direction crossing four rough fields and four painted or gated stiles or broken walls. In the fifth field bear right to cross a stile.

23. Turn left down a minor road and in a few metres join another road. Keep straight on to Grangemill ¹/₄ mile. Turn left onto the B5056 passing *The Hollybush Inn* on your right. Cross the A5012 and continue up the B5056 Ashbourne to Longcliffe road. In about 275 metres bear right up a minor road opposite the 'Works Access' sign.

24. Follow this road for nearly $^1/_2$ mile to a footpath post on the right. Turn right through a stile and walk up the field keeping a wall close on your right and passing under power lines. Cross a stile near a field corner and keep straight on.

25. Pass through a line of trees, turn left to follow the tree line for about 100 metres then turn right across the field to the opposite wall. Turn left to follow it uphill to cross a stile in the field corner.

26. Join a rough farm track, walk up through the farmyard to join the road. Turn right to follow the road through Aldwark, ignore a road upon the left. Pass a row of water troughs on your left and further on Lydgate Farm on your right. Just beyond the farm, ignore another road on the left. After about 100 metres turn right over the stile at the 'Footpath Winster $1^1/_2$' sign.

27. Walk down the field heading for a wall which climbs the opposite hillside to the left of Green Low. Pass through a gateway; there is a stone building on your left.

28. Bear right up the rough field to have the wall mentioned in no. 27 on your right. Pass by an old gate and keep straight on up the next two fields, over one stile then through a wall gap to cross a fenced grass track and over a fence stile.

29. Bear very slightly right down the field with the large quarry on your right. Pass through a wall gap, continue bearing right to cross a double stile near the field corner.

30. Bear left then almost immediately turn right up a wide fenced and walled grass track, following a line of trees on your right. At the end of the tree line cross a stile by a gate on your left. Follow the fence, wall and wood on your right down to cross a stile onto the A5012.

31. Cross the road to go through a stile by a 'Footpath' sign. Walk through a small rough area then keep straight on up to the top right-hand corner of a large field. Cross a squeeze stile above a copse of trees.

32. Bear very slightly left across the next field to cross a stile just above an old gateway; cross a track (Stunstead Lane) and go through the gated stile. Walk up the next field to the top left-hand corner, passing under power lines and crossing a gated stile, then on up to another power line to pass through a waymarked stile.

33. Bear slightly right up the next large field to cross a squeeze stile near the field corner. Cross the corners of the next 2 fields.

34. Continue in the same direction walking towards a copse of trees and crossing stiles or broken walls, a track and 4 fields. In the last field bear right to cross the stile by the footpath post.

34. Turn left down the road back to the car.

YOULGREAVE - WALK 18   9 MILES

LATHKILL DALE

**Limestone Way, Monyash - Lathkill Dale -
Meadow Place Farm - Moor Lane Car Park.**

MAP: O.S. Explorer OL. 24 The Peak District White Peak Area

DIRECTIONS: With Youlgreave church on your left drive through the village and just past *The Bull's Head* on your left bear right at a tall circular well dated 1829. (Notice the tiny old building known as Thimble Hall.) A few yards further on at a T-junction turn right up Moor Lane. In one mile turn left into Moor Lane car park. Grid Ref. S.K.194644.

DESCRIPTION: The walk starts with a section of the Limestone Way which crosses well-signposted upland pastures before descending into Cales Dale and then on up to One Ash Grange. In Monyash is *The Bull's Head* pub, a good refreshment stop. From here the walk follows 3$\frac{1}{2}$ miles of the beautiful and popular Lathkill Dale where there are many picnic spots. From the Dale, below Over Haddon, the route is well signposted along field paths back to the car park. If you wish to shorten the walk to 5$\frac{1}{2}$ miles, continue on down Cales Dale by turning right at the T-junction in instruction no. 7 and follow the path down to a footbridge which you cross and then turn right to follow the path down Lathkill Dale, then follow instructions 14 (last 2 sentences) - 18.

HISTORY: Monyash was once a centre of the Quaker Movement and of lead mining in the High Peak. Opposite *The Bull's Head* is the remains of an old market cross (1340). The farm at One Ash Grange, near the village, was once used by the monks of Roche Abbey. The remains of pigsties and a cave, possibly used for cooling cheese, can still be seen alongside our route.

Youlgreave, from the medieval translation Yellow Grove, dates from Norman times. The stained glass windows in the parish church are very fine examples of work by Kempe, William Morris and Burne-Jones. Well dressings are held here on the Saturday nearest to St. John the Baptist Day (June 24th).

ROUTE INSTRUCTIONS:

1. Leave the car park via the main vehicular entrance and turn left. In 130 metres cross the secondary road and go over the gated stile signposted 'Monyash'.

2. Walk diagonally left across the field. Cross a wall stile then cross the corner of the next field and go over another gated stile.

3. Follow the well-defined path across the middle of the large field ahead. Cross a fence stile and continue in the same direction to go through a gate and walk through a copse. Go over a corner stile.

4. Walk diagonally across the next field towards Calling Low Farm. Go through a small swing gate following the 'Diverted Footpath' sign. Keep straight on to go through a gate on your left.

5. Go through 3 swing gates following a well-defined path.

6. Cross the corner of the next field and go through another small gate. Follow a well-defined path down the next three fields and through three small gates.

7. Go down the steep stepped path into Cales Dale. Cross the stile and bear left uphill to a T-junction of paths and turn left. Follow the path below the limestone cliffs as it climbs out of the dale.

8. Cross a stile and continue ahead up towards One Ash Grange Farm. Follow a wall on your left then cross a stile, at the top of steps, by a black barn.

9. Pass between barns and follow the farm track. Notice the cave, possibly used for cooling cheese, and mediaeval piggeries on your right. Continue to follow the farm track as it bends round to the right through a gateway and then uphill ignoring the track upon the left.

10. At the top of the track go through a gate and turn left to walk up the field keeping a wall close on your left. Cross a stile on your left near the field corner. Turn right, now following the wall on your right.

11. Go through a small gate in the field corner and continue on down the next field to go through a squeeze stile. Cross the top end of Fern Dale then bear right to go over the wall stile ahead. Turn left and in a few metres go over a stile by a gate to enter a walled track.

12. Follow this track for about $^1/_2$ mile. At the road junction turn right for a few yards to join the village road. Walk into Monyash passing the Green and pond on the right. At the crossroads (B5055) turn right. Pass *The Bull's Head* on your left and continue to walk through the village.

13. About 375 metres out of the village at the bottom of the hill turn right by the public toilets to go through a gate into Lathkill Dale.

14. At first you follow a wide grass path crossing 2 stiles and 1 gate, then you enter a narrow rocky section of the dale with its steep limestone sides and cross two stiles. Eventually you reach a large cavern on your right, from which the river Lathkill flows after a period of heavy rain. Now follow a wider woodland path by the river. You will walk a total of nearly $3^1/_2$ miles down Lathkill Dale.

15. Pass through the stile by the gate and bear right for a few metres down to a minor road at Lathkill Lodge. Turn right and cross the footbridge over the river (if it is flowing!). Turn left and follow the wide woodland track uphill.